ENGLISH POLITICAL PLURALISM

NUMBER 2 OF THE
COLUMBIA STUDIES IN PHILOSOPHY
EDITED UNDER THE DEPARTMENT OF
PHILOSOPHY, COLUMBIA UNIVERSITY

Henry Meyer Magid

ENGLISH POLITICAL PLURALISM ~ The Problem Of Freedom and Organization

NEW YORK: MORNINGSIDE HEIGHTS
COLUMBIA UNIVERSITY PRESS

1941

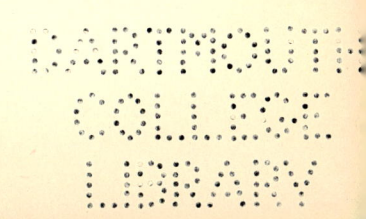

COPYRIGHT 1941

COLUMBIA UNIVERSITY PRESS, NEW YORK

Foreign agents: OXFORD UNIVERSITY PRESS, Humphrey Milford, Amen House, London, E.C. 4, England, and B. I. Building, Nicol Road, Bombay, India; MARUZEN COMPANY, Ltd., 6 Nihonbashi, Tori-Nichome, Tokyo, Japan

MANUFACTURED IN THE UNITED STATES OF AMERICA

To
MY MOTHER and MY FATHER

ACKNOWLEDGMENTS

I wish to acknowledge my deep indebtedness to Professor H. W. Schneider, of Columbia University, for his sustaining interest and advice throughout the writing of this book; to Professors J. H. Randall, Jr., and Ernest Nagel, of Columbia University; and to Dr. Eric Hula, of the Graduate Faculty of Political and Social Science of the New School for Social Research, all of whom read the manuscript and offered many helpful suggestions.

I wish to thank the editors of *Ethics* and the University of Chicago Press for permission to use an article by me, "Freedom and Political Unity," which appeared in *Ethics* in January, 1941, and also the following publishers and publications for allowing me to quote from their books or periodicals: George Bell & Sons, Thornton Butterworth, Harcourt, Brace and Company, Little, Brown and Company, Longmans, Green and Co., The Macmillan Company, Methuen & Co., *The New Republic,* W. W. Norton & Company, Ohio State University Press, Oxford University Press, Leonard Parsons, and Frederick A. Stokes Company.

Henry M. Magid

New York City
April 3, 1941

CONTENTS

1. Introduction   3
2. *Figgis:* The Significance of the Real Personality of Groups   10
3. *Cole:* A Pluralistic Theory of Guild Socialism   31
4. *Laski:* Individualistic Pluralism   47
5. Conclusion   63
    Bibliography   93
    Index   97

ENGLISH POLITICAL
PLURALISM

1.

INTRODUCTION

The figures in the movement that has come to be known as "political pluralism" are numerous and widely distributed, geographically, politically, and academically. The movement has included thinkers in several European countries, as well as in the United States. Its doctrines have been used or misused by the left, the center, and the right. Its position has been stated by lawyers, churchmen, economists, politicians, and political philosophers. Historical accounts of it trace its sources in various fields back to William James (philosophy), the Middle Ages and Otto von Gierke's studies of them (law), a papal encyclical of Leo XIII, various church movements in nineteenth-century England, and syndicalism (politics).

In the only book-length study of political pluralism [1] Hsiao attempts to indicate the sources of the movement and to state and criticize the various forms of the doctrine. In general he sees political pluralism as a criticism of abstract monism and, in that respect as valid. But he asserts that pluralism, as it was elaborated positively, was also an abstract doctrine. Its inadequacies indicate that what is necessary, and possible as a result of the

[1] Hsiao, *Political Pluralism*.

INTRODUCTION

pluralistic criticism of abstract monism, is a "concrete" monism. For Hsiao, Hegel anticipated such a doctrine. It is almost superfluous to point out that if freedom is our interest a concrete pluralism might be still better. Although Hsiao considers freedom one of the themes of pluralism, he does not make sufficiently clear that it was in relation to its analysis of this problem that pluralism made its chief contribution to the problem of the democratic state.

Other critics of the movement usually begin by acknowledging that there is a great deal to be learned from the criticism leveled by the pluralists at the doctrine of state sovereignty. Once this is granted, the critics take up one or more of three lines of attack. (1) Pluralism leads to disastrous practical consequences.[2] (2) The pluralists have failed to provide an adequate complement to or substitute for the criticized doctrine of sovereignty, that is, they have not developed an adequate theory of the state.[3] (3) Pluralism means the destruction of law, and hence of the state.[4] It is not my purpose to refute these criticisms, but rather to try to look at pluralism from another point of view.

Political pluralism, as a conscious movement, attempted to reconsider the concepts of political philosophy in the light of changing social conditions. It focused attention on the increasing power and autonomy of various groups in society. It sought to find out the implications of this growth for the state. To understand

[2] Ellis, "The Pluralistic State," *American Political Science Review*, XIV (August, 1920), 393–407.
[3] Coker, "Pluralistic Theories and the Attack upon State Sovereignty," in Merriam and Barnes, *A History of Political Theories, Recent Times*, pp. 80–119.
[4] Elliot, *The Pragmatic Revolt in Politics*, pp. 142–66.

INTRODUCTION

the doctrines developed by the pluralists it is necessary to consider their problems, their methods, and the results of both. Underlying the work of the men to be considered here, was a passionate interest in freedom. As Englishmen they claimed it as their heritage. Today it is our problem. The aim of this essay is to investigate the theories of the English pluralistic movement in order to discover its contribution to an analysis of freedom. Since this is not primarily a historical study, it is not necessary to consider all the figures in English pluralism or to make exhaustive studies of those considered. Figgis, Cole, and Laski have been chosen because, in the first place, they are the most prominent figures in the movement and, in the second place, they represent different approaches. Figgis was interested in the problem of the church in society; Cole's interests were mainly economic; and Laski's were political and legal.[5]

That there was a pluralistic movement in England and that it took the particular form that it did were the results of a series of particular factors in the previous history of political and philosophical thought in England, as well as of the social history of the nation. As a political theory the pluralist movement was a reaction against the idealistic "theory of the state." Idealism found its way into political theory in the first place because of the inadequacy of the old liberalism of the Utilitarian school. The old liberalism led to a sort of atomic individualism and was responsible for setting the individ-

[5] "Meanwhile a movement, possibly academic and not of any great extent, seems to be setting towards the vindication of the rights of the religious group; and we may perhaps detect in Dr. Figgis the ally in the religious sphere of the policy which in the economic sphere appears as Guild Socialism, and in the political sphere as the new Liberalism."—Barker, *Political Thought from Spencer to Today*, p. 182.

[5]

INTRODUCTION

ual against the state. Herbert Spencer's work merely carried that way of thinking to its logical conclusion. The stream of the old liberalism dried up. As Barker put it, "not a modification of the old Benthamite premises, but a new philosophy was needed." [6] What was needed was a new philosophy that could give coherence to political thinking—something that could get the theory of the state together again. Idealism, imported from Germany, where the sense of order and organization was strong, was amply suited for that purpose. The work of Bradley, Green, and Bosanquet shows what sort of miracle can be wrought with a combination of the English liberal temper and the German philosophy of organization.

In spite of this new philosophy of the state, pressing problems of political action were not being solved. While these new philosophies may have possessed a certain consistency, their effect in practice on the continent began to be alarming. It was felt that action had to be taken to preserve freedom in the face of the growing centralization of the state. Those with common or like interests formed groups for the furtherance of their interests and to make their voices count amid the clamor of other interests. There had been such groups before, various dissenting churches in England for example, and when they were strong they were a more vital factor in determining the actions of men in the community than the government or the state. So it was now. The voices of the various churches, the trade unions, the professional associations, and even the economic classes began to be heard. These voices became louder and more in-

[6] *Ibid.*, pp. 10–11.

INTRODUCTION

sistent. Something had to be done, in theory as well as in practice. Practice muddled along and gradually came to recognize these groups. Ways were sought to give them representation and to satisfy their demands. Some problems were solved; many were not. Meanwhile, as a necessary consequence, theory was undergoing a change.

The old individualism had failed because it did not satisfy the need for unity in society.[7] The idealism that followed it began by postulating that unity and deriving an organization of society from it. But those who looked saw that there was no inner unity. It helped little to say that there would be unity if people were more perspicacious and that hence the unity was really there. The insistence on unity in the absence of unity tended either to the destruction of freedom or to irrelevant speculation. Social and political problems were pressing, and men were willing to take advantage of the practical opportunities that were at hand instead of waiting for the sanction of theory. This had its effect on theory. It was recognized that it was important that political theory have, besides consistency, some relevance to things as they are and can be, not merely to things as they would be "if" or as they ought to be on the basis of some eternal principle. If there are elements of unity in society, all well and good. The task is to find them. If not, what is to be gained by postulating them?

This change in attitude, which amounted to a revolution in political theory for those who underwent it, had as one of its results the pluralistic movement in political theory. It was a revolution, because all the basic terms of political thinking were scrutinized in a way which left

[7] *Ibid.*

INTRODUCTION

few of them with their old stature and prestige. A new and more "realistic" way of thinking about politics was the result. It is this change in attitude and its results that I shall attempt to consider in this essay.

The relevance of a study of the English political pluralists to present problems is not difficult to see. Today the state is taking on greater and greater power. This means that familiar liberties are being threatened. One could view the pluralistic movement as a futile attempt to stave off the inevitable. Indeed, that may be the verdict of future historians. Meanwhile, if we deny the inevitability of totalitarianism, we may discover in pluralism, on the one hand, an attempt to analyze the problem of freedom in the light of modern world conditions—those same conditions which for others necessarily involve totalitarianism—and, on the other hand, an attempt to define and organize the plurality of powers and pressure groups operative in society—an attempt which grew directly out of the pluralist's attempt to conceive authority pluralistically.

It was not just a theory of the state that the work of Figgis, Cole, and Laski elaborated. It was rather a series of attempts to show in what senses we can be free in modern society. This exposition of the ways in which freedom manifests itself and under what conditions is what I call the problem of freedom. In practice this "problem" breaks down into many particular problems of freedom—each with its own set of persons and interests in a particular environment. What this essay attempts to do is to show that a general structure can be discovered in modern society in which freedom is given institutional embodiment as a useful theoretical framework for the analysis of particular problems of freedom.

INTRODUCTION

Institutional freedom so conceived is in a position between the idealistic conception of individual autonomy (Laski) and bills of rights which rely on judicial protection of specific liberties.

2. *Figgis:*
THE SIGNIFICANCE OF THE REAL PERSONALITY OF GROUPS

It is advantageous to start the discussion of political pluralism in England with John Neville Figgis, because he is a connecting link between previous pluralistic tendencies and the movement as it subsequently developed. He leaned more directly on Gierke than later writers, who in turn depended on him. It is in Figgis that we find as clearly as anywhere both the motives of the pluralists and the kinds of problem that arise out of the theory that they developed.[1]

Like many another pluralist, Figgis speaks chiefly in the interest of one group, a church, and his purpose is to show under what circumstances that group can secure the conditions necessary for its free development.[2] Thus the writings of Figgis center in the problem of freedom of association. His work may be divided into two parts:

[1] Hsiao's treatment of Figgis is limited to scattered references in footnotes (*op. cit.*, pp. 34n, 36n, 47n, 50n, 62n, 78n, 136n, 212n). He considers him merely as one who applied Gierke's view to the problem of the church. The present analysis will indicate how the problem of freedom colored Figgis's view and made it clearly distinguishable from Gierke's.

[2] An appreciation of Figgis's view of the nature of a church is fundamental to any understanding of his political position. He says: "Once more the notion of individualist Christianity is foreign to the Gospel. That religion which teaches the fatherhood of God and the brotherhood

first, an elaboration of the meaning and importance of freedom of association; second, a consideration of the implications of it for a theory of the state.

The starting point of Figgis's theory of associations, as well as of much of the idealistic political theory in England, is that the best structure of society is that which gives the individual the opportunity for self-development.[3] This criterion is to be distinguished from justice and from natural law, for this theory attempts to get beyond justice and natural law to the process of growth, in terms of which they can be defined teleologically. The concept of self-development, or the realization of self, especially as elaborated by Green, has to a certain extent done this.

The introduction of the term "self-realization" into the discussion was intended to turn attention toward concrete questions which can be investigated empirically. In this way the idealistic theory of Green, which asked,

---

of man, of which the cardinal maxim is to love God and one another, must inevitably be the most penetrating of all forms of social union. What Christianity does is to carry to their full conclusion the implications of human nature and the lessons of political union. The faith which is the living expression of mutual love cannot be satisfied by a society which subsists on a basis of contract, with the individual free to leave it while still remaining a full Christian. Love is the most penetrating of all forces. It unites the spirits, of men, not merely their minds. Where it is real, it expresses itself in a mutuality of intercourse which is deeper than can be put into words and changes the whole personality. We must not figure the membership of a Church like a heap of pebbles which are unchanged as they lie together; rather is it union of many diverse elements, all constantly changing and acting upon each other."
—*The Fellowship of the Mystery*, pp. 53–54.

[3] The notion of self-development is something like the notion of self-realization as used by the idealists. However, Figgis does not indicate how far he goes with the idealists in the metaphysical, psychological, and ethical elaboration of this concept. The use made of it in political theory is what is relevant here (*vide infra*).

in considering a given institution, whether it is conducive to the self-realization of individuals, was a preparatory step for the pluralistic view. While Green used this theory to show that the only possible function of the state is negative—hindering hindrances to self-realization—Figgis used it, together with the premise that it is chiefly in groups such as churches that individuals realize themselves, to show the vital place of the group in society. The deduction from these two postulates is that unless groups are allowed free development the self-development of individuals will be hindered.

It can be seen that there is one point in Figgis's argument which requires further elaboration. On the basis of the two postulates mentioned above, the most that Figgis can say is that groups are necessary for self-development. He wants to say more. He wants to say that a certain kind of group is necessary for self-development, namely, a free and unhindered group. We must consider the grounds for this contention.

Groups, according to Figgis, can be viewed in two ways. Either they can be considered as living and organic, with a principle of growth within them, or they can be considered as wholes in appearance only and in reality as merely parts of a larger whole. If they are viewed in the first way they are held to be "real persons." Figgis's argument amounts to an insistence that the real personality of groups must be realized in order not to prevent the self-realization of individuals. If he could have shown this, he would have proved his case; but the most that he was able to show was that free associations (by analogy with a free church) are necessary for the development of the real personality of associations, for the self-realization of *groups*.

Since the nature of the "true society" or association is the crux of the matter, it will be advantageous to determine in more detail just what the true conception of an association is as contrasted with the false conception. Figgis makes this abundantly clear in the first chapter of *Churches in the Modern State,* especially in dealing with the case of the amalgamation of the Free Kirk and the United Presbyterians in Scotland. It is a false conception of an association, to take the negative side of the argument first, which holds that an association, that is, a church, is bound by its original document of organization, or is merely a creation of the state, or is an aggregate of individuals treated as a single person for convenience, or has no mind or will of its own. If any of these descriptions of group life were accurate, the Austinian theory of law would be tenable, and the decision of the House of Lords in the case of the *Free Church of Scotland Appeals* would have had a basis in fact.[4] But, says Figgis, the very fact that the decision of the Lords proved unworkable indicates that it was not based on a true conception of the nature of corporate life. If the Lords had had a true conception, they would have realized that a church, since it is a true society, has a mind and a will of its own, has a principle of inherent life, which means that it is not bound by the dead hand of its original document—in short, is a living body which can define and develop its own doctrine.[5]

This indicates that when you establish self-realization as the criterion by which you judge an institution, you

[4] "Let us return to the case of the Scotch Churches. Does it not seem as though there must be something fundamentally erroneous in a decision which proved so practically unworkable as that of the House of Lords?"—*Churches in the Modern State,* p. 32.
[5] *Ibid.*, pp. 22, 33, 36, *et passim.*

are not thereby specifying any given structure of society. The political and social theory that you develop depends on whose self-realization you are interested in and how you define that self-realization. Contrast Figgis and Bosanquet. Self-realization was a starting point for both men. For Figgis, who emphasized the importance of the religious liberty to believe what you will, it resulted in the theory of freedom of groups. For Bosanquet, who emphasized reason, it implied a theory of the organic nature of freedom as well as of society.

For Figgis the freedom and the real personality of an association go hand in hand. Their implications can best be considered in terms of the following questions: How are individuals related to groups? How are groups related to the state and to each other? What, indeed, is the structure of the state as far as Figgis outlines it?

In Figgis's terms the problems can be stated thus: Given an adequate view of human life in society, what follows concerning the nature of associations and their relationship to that *communitas communitatum* called the state? In other words, what follows concerning the nature of society, if you start with freedom of association as the basic premise? In the course of the elaboration of his argument just what he means by the "nature of human life in society" becomes clearer.

Although he was mainly interested in the church, Figgis was careful to point out the wider aspect of the problem. The church is merely one of a class of societies, and this brings him to the general problem of the "structure of civil society and the nature of political union." [6] In general we have seen that the true conception of the nature of associations involves the recognition of their

[6] *Ibid.*, p. 40.

real personality—that is, of their freedom. A real person is free in that he is living, organic, and not derived. Figgis pursues the analogy between corporate persons and natural persons—two species of the genus "real person." On the one hand, just as the state does not originate natural persons, so it does not originate corporate persons. On the other hand, just as the state regulates the existence of and the relations between natural persons, so it will regulate in certain respects the existence of and relations between corporate persons and between the former and the latter. This makes a pretty analogy, even to the point where, though Figgis neglects to mention it, in both cases (that of natural as well as that of corporate persons) the limit of the state's power over individuals is the thorniest of all problems. If the limit of the state's power over individuals were clear, Figgis might have accomplished more with his analogy; but this was and is just as much up in the air as was the problem that especially concerned Figgis. An indication of this is the fact that Figgis is very clear as to the implications of the false view of these smaller societies. It leads to tyranny, which is their destruction. But he has trouble, and this trouble is the chief characteristic of his book, in dealing with the implications of the true conception of associations.

Taking up now the implications of this analysis for political theory, Figgis considers some of the faults of the traditional conception which treated the state as "The Great Leviathan." This traditional doctrine of the absolute sovereignty of the state stems in theory, he claims, from the notion of the unity of the state. Once you assume that the state must be a unity, you can deduce that it must have a unified authority, and so forth. Besides the practical objection that this leads to tyranny, the more important objection for the purposes of this essay is the theoretical one that it does violence to the facts of social life. The absolutist theory makes possible the clear-cut distinction between things that are public and things that are private. Everything related to the state is public; everything else is private. Figgis, following Gierke, takes issue with this distinction in the name of associations. Man, whose personality is social, develops that personality in numerous groups that cannot be said to be derived from the state and yet are obviously not private. Either we must widen our notion of those things that are public, so as to include those groups other than the state, or we must invent a new category for such associations. Figgis does the former by recognizing the real personality of those groups. The performance of similar functions with regard to the individual puts those associations in the same category as the state. "The relations between a member and his society are more akin to those of a citizen to a State than to anything in the individual." [7] Figgis uses another argument against Austinianism—an argument, however, which is valid only for the church as he conceived it. "Under such a view, there can be no possible place for the religious body in the sense of a Church living a supernatural life, and the claim is quite just that no Church should have any standard of morals different from those of the State." [8] Although Figgis does not lay stress on this point, I feel that it gives an indication of another source of his attack on the notion of the complete sovereignty of the state. There is something morally wrong in it.

On the positive side Figgis develops the argument for

[7] *Ibid.*, p. 69.   [8] *Ibid.*, p. 68.

freedom. He points out that in former times those who fought for freedom fought for freedom to rule without hindrance.[9] Now that the political authority of the state is supreme, those in the camp of freedom are interested in freedom from the control of that political power. The way toward that freedom is decentralization—that is, the recognition of the real personality of groups. Figgis specifically says that the problem is not that of individual freedom.[10] The fight for individual liberty is of no avail, since on the one hand it pits the individual against the state and on the other hand, even if gained, without corporate liberty it is ineffective in practice, since self-realization is achieved in groups.

Thus Figgis attempts to show that from whatever point of view we approach the theory of the state—self-realization, relevance to the facts of social life, liberty—we find the Austinian theory lacking because it assumes unity and the sharp distinction between public and private. In every case he puts forward as the solution the recognition of the real personality and public character of associations.

He presents two positive arguments showing the advisability of recognizing real personality. In the first place, this recognition is the only way to preserve freedom. Failure to recognize real personality leads to tyranny. On the other hand, since it is a social fact, you cannot long go on denying its existence.

Whatever other influences may have assisted in forming the minds of the judges, the truth is that the judgment bears witness to the fact that corporate personality, this unity of life

---

[9] Figgis here refers to the conflict between church and state in the Middle Ages (*ibid.*, pp. 78–79).
[10] *Ibid.*, p. 58.

and action, is a thing which grows up naturally and inevitably in bodies of men united for a permanent end, and that it cannot in the long run be denied merely by the process of saying that it is not there.[11]

He brings the two points together in the following summary:

It is, in a word, a real life and personality which those bodies are forced to claim, which we believe that they possess by the nature of the case, and not by the arbitrary grant of the sovereign. To deny this real life is to be false to the facts of social existence, and is of the same nature as that denial of human personality which we call slavery, and is always in its nature unjust and tyrannical.[12]

Taken separately, these arguments appeal to different groups. The first is directed toward those who are interested in preserving freedom. The second demands no such interest, but appeals generally to all interested in seeing government work. If the second is sound, the first is unnecessary. In fact, if you take them literally, the second contradicts the first. Either the denial of real and inherent life to associations is impossible, or it will lead to tyranny. In general Figgis places more weight on the fear of tyranny. Relying largely on idealism's respect for persons, he has faith that the bare recognition of groups as persons will prevent tyranny. But even the most real person is not safe from a tyrant.

However much we might value a complete theory of the state from Figgis's hand, we look for it in vain; his special interests prevent him from undertaking such a task in his book, *Churches in the Modern State* (which deals with churches more than with the modern state), and he never elsewhere amplified his views on this sub-

[11] *Ibid.*, p. 64.   [12] *Ibid.*, p. 42.

ject. The nature of his special interest forces him, however, to indicate what a view of the state based on the recognition of the real personality of societies would be like. It is worth pursuing these indications and considering what problems they raise.

For Figgis the function of the state is to regulate relations between individuals and between groups and individuals and between groups. His indiscriminate use of the terms "government" and "state" indicates that he did not distinguish between them.[13] The problem of the "free state" is to perform this regulating function without destroying the freedom necessary for self-realization. He discusses the problem in terms of religious self-realization. If we take the simplest case, that of a religious homogeneity in society, the problem of government is simple. Since everyone would believe in the same church, an established church is possible, and there can be a fully integrated society. Freedom would cease to be a problem, except possibly for a few religious dissenters; or, rather, it would be a different kind of problem—one which would issue, as in the Middle Ages, in a conflict between the church and the state as to who was to be free to rule. Unfortunately for so simple a solution, the condition in which this was an accurate statement of the problem of freedom no longer exists. The situation we meet today (and Figgis insists we have to accept it as setting our problem) is one of religious heterogeneity. There are many churches, and because of their multiplicity they have become weak in relation to the state which has become more unified. The problem now concerns the relations of the numerous churches to each other and to the state. Figgis finds that those on the side

[13] *Ibid.*, p. 103.

of the state feel that the state should be the supreme authority in all church matters. He cannot admit this, because he holds that the church, every real church, is a "real person" and would cease to be one, just as the individual would become a slave, if ruled in every particular by the state. Leaving out of account extreme Ultramontanism, the polar opposite of statism is the position that holds that the church should be entirely free from any control by the state. Figgis must reject this view as well, since it leads to corporate anarchy and the breakdown of civil society. Thus his position is a compromise. The state is to control the church in certain respects, and the church is to be free in others.

What is the nature of this compromise? Just as the state in Figgis's time recognized the personality of individuals and yet in certain respects regulated them, so it must recognize and regulate the church, that is, the church is not outside the law. In the case of individuals regulation is necessary to protect individual rights; in the case of groups regulation is necessary to protect corporate rights. In determining which actions of the group can be controlled by the state and which are independent of it he sets up two realms of action, making a distinction analogous to that of Mill in his argument for individual freedom. Although Figgis rejects this distinction of Mill,[14] his own distinction is similar to it. A group can perform two kinds of act: the first act concerns merely its own affairs; the second impinges on people outside the group. In the former case the rules that hold are valid merely for members of the group and owe their authority to the authority of the association over its members. In the latter case the rules that hold are the rules

[14] *Ibid.*, p. 110.

of law proper and are enforceable by the civic power. What this means for the individual, who is usually a member both of a church and of a state, is that for some actions he is accountable only to the church, for others to both church and state, and for still others only to the state.

While Figgis rejects, because of the complications due to religious heterogeneity, the Catholic position of the Encyclical *Immortale Dei* of Leo XIII (1885) that there are two perfect societies composed of the same members, nevertheless he says that this is more nearly correct than most current views, and indeed his own view, *mutatis mutandis,* seems to be almost identical with it.

He is not afraid to carry out the implications of this view which achieves a free church in a "free state" by giving the church one sphere of freedom and the state another. He insists that in asking the state not to interfere in matters that concern only the church, churchmen must be willing to refrain from advocating any political program in the name of the church, however they may feel as citizens.

The practical objections to this view are obvious enough. Who is to decide what belongs to the sphere of the church and what to the state can be debated. Figgis would answer that the state is to decide on the basis of the recognition of real personality. But this does not solve the problem. Who is to decide whether real personality has been violated? Figgis gives no clear answer to this question.

Another and, I feel, equally formidable objection has to do with the special interest of Figgis. His argument is carried on mainly in terms of the church, but he continually insists that it has a wider bearing and that it applies to all other groups, including trade unions. Would he be willing to admit the vital connection between freedom of trade unions and the self-realization of individuals? Furthermore, in the case of the church it is relatively simple to distinguish between actions that concern only the church and those that have a wider bearing. In the case of the trade union it is practically impossible, since the purpose of a trade union is to deal with another group. And, if the trade union raises difficulties, what of the various irreconcilable groups, such as the Communist Party? Have they no mind and will of their own? Are they to be treated as true societies?

Evidently there is a problem here in addition to the question of the recognition of true or free societies. Admitting that a given association is a true society, the problem still remains to what degree its life is interrelated with the life of other groups, especially with the state. Even though metaphysically the freedom of groups is admitted as a fact, problems of their coördination, regulation, and conflict still remain. This raises a different problem of freedom and regulation and concerns liberty, not inherent, but granted by the state.

In an essay entitled "The Discredited State" [15] Ernest Barker attempted to criticize the doctrine of the real personality of groups as Figgis expounded it. First, he pointed out, as Maitland and Figgis had pointed out before him, that groups had always flourished in England, whatever their genus name. He concedes that the fight for freedom was carried on mainly by these groups. Moreover, he indicates the connection between the emphasis on the rights of groups and the old doctrine of natural rights. But all this is preliminary.

[15] *Political Quarterly*, No. 5 (Feb., 1915), 101–21.

His criticism of the doctrine of real personality is on philosophic grounds. When we use the expression "real person" in relation to a group, we are using a universal. In criticism of Figgis, Barker raises certain objections to "real person" as a satisfactory designation for groups. He admits, first, that for purposes of law there is much to be said for it. In that field it is efficacious for growth. But if the term is used more widely, it raises a host of unnecessary problems. There is no pragmatic reason why we have to worry about the nature and location of the transcendent wills of groups. What Barker had in mind was that once we hypostatize a technical legal expression into a metaphysical entity, we begin to talk about words instead of things. For this reason Barker suggests the neutral and almost colorless expression "organizing idea." Thus he introduces his own terminology and his idealistic prejudices. Men, he says, continually organize themselves around ideas. The people concerned with any one organizing idea change, but the idea remains. The personality of the people may change as a result of an organizing idea, but this does not mean that a new superpersonality has been born. Furthermore, organizing ideas may be altered. If this happens, he says, "we do not kill a personality that existed before, or create a personality that did not exist before: we alter our organizing idea." [16]

[16] Barker, *op. cit.*, p. 111. Barker goes into the question of real personality in law. Law has many rubrics or titles for the group—"trust, contract, *persona ficta* or real person" (p. 112). The first three of these rubrics he rejects on the ground that they are not conducive to the growth of groups. Maitland pointed out (*Collected Papers*, III, 321–404) that it was through the use of the concept of "trust" that groups were able to flourish in England. Figgis refers to this essay by Maitland. If "trust" is to be rejected, it is on other grounds than that it prevents the growth of groups (Figgis, p. 67). All this, of course, assumes that the growth of groups is a good thing. Figgis, Barker, and the rest of the pluralists considered it a sign of a healthy society.

Barker has two main objections to real personality. (1) What happens to a real personality when its organizing idea is altered? Is it killed and a new one born? The question is not quite fair, since, in asking it, Barker assumes his own theory of groups. In Figgis's language, the matter is quite simple. The fact that the doctrines of groups change, whereas the groups remain, is natural and to be expected, since they are living bodies and life means development and growth. It is only when an outside force, like the state, tries to change a corporate body, that it is killed. (2) The concept of real personality implies for Barker intrinsic value, and on this basis all real personality should be fostered. But what of Mafia and Camorra? Should they be allowed self-realization? This is Barker's standard objection,[17] but it is valid only insofar as it applies to the idea of self-realization in general. Figgis might reply that such "groups" are not genuine precisely because they are, not instruments of self-realization, but its enemies. In any case, a group must be willing to submit to legitimate regulation, a rule which would eliminate secret, criminal, and predatory societies. It can be added that when Barker says "one can argue with ideas: one can show that they are partial or erroneous; one can deflate a bubble idea with a prick of logic" [18] he underestimates the effort required to cope with Mafia or Camorra or the state. You can't kill groups so easily with argument.

Figgis's qualified approval of the Catholic position and his continued setting of the church against the state indicate the need for a further consideration of the theoretical problems involved in his use of the expressions "ascend-

[17] *Ibid.*, p. 113; also *Political Thought from Spencer to Today*, p. 179.
[18] "The Discredited State," p. 113.

ing hierarchy of groups" and *"communitas communitatum."* The central difficulties emerge in a comparison of Figgis and Barker on these points. Figgis had asserted that he found what Barker refers to as a "graded hierarchy of organizing ideas." [19] Barker asks, is there such an hierarchy? In answer to this Figgis would say that certain groups are more important than others and that there must be a group to regulate groups. Yet actually, Barker points out, no one organizing idea has always been supreme. Even that general group formed by public opinion, the broadest group Barker can think of, has defects, since it represents only the opinion of the majority and in any case is never homogeneous. There are many organizing ideas, and not always, in fact rarely, does the broadest one command the greatest loyalty in a crucial situation. The broader idea is likely to be an abstraction or a compromise.

Barker finds it difficult to conceive where we are to find one inclusive organizing idea. To say that one exists now and is called "the state" is absurd. The exact status of the idea of the state varies with time and place. The trouble with Austinian sovereignty is that it, too, is a concept, and reality is wider than a concept. "It substitutes unitarianism for federalism, a corner in lieu of a competition." [20] The position Barker ends with is what he refers to as polyarchism, with the state *primus inter pares*. There are many organizing ideas, and they grow, compete, and perhaps die. The state represents the idea of law and order. It, too, has its ups and downs. At the time when Barker wrote, the state was being discredited in theory in the name of groups. This attitude indicates to him that there is a firm foundation in law and order.

[19] *Ibid.*, p. 114.   [20] *Ibid.*, p. 120.

But, he says, "If that basis is not secure, if the building of our common life shows signs and cracks of subsidences, if the enemy without should see a gaping opportunity for his battering ram, the cry of 'Back to law and order' will be great, and will prevail." [21] The strengthening of the state in times of war and threatened revolution verifies his prediction.

As contrasted with this, we must see what sort of case Figgis makes for the state as a real personality and in what its freedom consists. Figgis could validly ascribe real personality to the state if it were known that the state has a business of its own and a will and a mind of its own to determine how it should act with regard to that business. The function of the state, according to Figgis, is to regulate the relations between groups and between groups and individuals. Whether that is the only business of the state Figgis does not say.

. . . and however strongly we may assert the naturalness of corporate life, no one, I believe would deny the duty of the State to demand proper proofs that it [a society] is being formed and supplied with duly constituted organs of its unity; while, further, it must clearly be within the province of the State to prevent bodies of persons acting secretly and practically as corporations, in order to escape rightful government control.[22]

This indicates that the state does more than merely adjust conflicts between groups; it regulates their very essence. If the state is a group as Barker and Figgis seem to hold, it is at least a different and stronger kind of group, whose business seems to be not to have any business of its own, but merely to serve to regulate other groups and relations between them. However, Figgis's insistence that men are

[21] *Ibid.*   [22] *Churches in the Modern State*, p. 103.

concerned with the affairs of the state only insofar as they are citizens suggests that it is not a *communitas communitatum*, as he claims, but a *communitas* of the citizens for the regulation of the *communitates*.

A regulating state of this kind might conceivably not be a real personality, since it would have no internal life of its own, unless all groups could be said to be internal to it. If this were granted, and if the regulating activity of the state were taken seriously, the real personality of the groups would be in danger.[23] Unless we can indicate quite clearly either a criterion for state interference or how, in the institutional set-up of the state, such a criterion is arrived at, we have not completely solved the problem of freedom as Figgis posed it. If the state decides, we are back at the old doctrine of the absolute sovereignty of the state; if it is up to the group, we must find a new theory of group individuality with which to describe the function of the state.

This attempt to elaborate the view of Figgis with regard to the state shows that there are two antithetic strains in his thought, and there is no reason to suppose that an ultimate reconciliation is possible. One strain is represented by the use of phrases such as *communitas communitatum* and an ascending hierarchy of groups. This strain is never elaborated and seems to be a residue of other ways of thinking. It might be traced to Gierke's organic theory of the state. If it is taken at its face value, it would seem to deny all the pluralism that Figgis is concerned with and point to a monistic view of the state

---

[23] Compare Hsiao, *op. cit.*, p. 36. Also the following by MacIver: "Observe nevertheless that Figgis speaks of the church *in* the state. The church of which he speaks in such otherwise clear terms is not *in* the state any more than the state is *in* the church. Both are within the community."—*The Modern State*, p. 170n.

on the basis of some pre-established harmony of functions. The other strain is that implied in his analysis of the real personality and the freedom of groups. This strain directs attention to the fact that there is no set order of groups, but merely the competition of groups in overlapping spheres; the state here becomes an adjuster of conflicts, only in this sense *primus inter pares,* whose main concern as a group or particular *communitas* of citizens is in law and order—that is, in regulating the external relations of groups to each other and to persons outside them. Barker, who rejects real personality as a political concept and who, therefore, is not involved in the problem of the real personality of the state, is able to take this position without destroying the basis of his analysis.

In the light of this analysis it is very easy to conclude that Figgis's whole attempt to state the conditions of a free church in a free state failed so far as the "free state" is concerned and to go further and say that all who start as he did are bound to fail. The practical problem is insoluble so long as the distinction between internal and external relations is dubious. However, there is another way to judge Figgis's achievement. By his very failure, he has succeeded in making quite clear just what the problem of the modern state is. The demand for absolute freedom is as indefensible as the demand for absolute sovereignty. At the same time that we insist on the right of groups to freedom because of the valuable fruits of that freedom, we must also realize the importance of the regulation of the groups in order to preserve peace among them and thereby secure to them their freedom. Where Figgis failed was in the terms in which he set the problem. His introduction of the concept of real personality as the basis of freedom carried over embarrassing philosophical commitments from idealism, as the comparison with Barker has shown, and his failure to elaborate the interrelations between freedom and regulation leaves us with a clear notion of the difficulty, but still groping for the solution.

What, then, is the relevance of Figgis for political pluralism? As an importer of Gierke he would at least have secondary place in the movement. But in his own right he has presented certain views which explain the regard in which he was held by those who in some way supported the pluralistic position from the point of view of idealism.

His most important claim to our attention comes from his arguments against the Austinian doctrine of absolute sovereignty. These arguments were repeated in one way or another, as suited their purpose, by all the figures in the pluralist movement. The core of the argument comes out in the following passage:

But it seems a weakness in a doctrine that you can only fit the facts into its framework by making such serious qualifications [as are necessary for the Austinian theory], and it would appear a more reasonable maxim to get a theory of law and government not by laying down an abstract doctrine of unity, but by observing the facts of life as it is lived, and trying to set down the actual features of civil society. What do we find as a fact? Not, surely, a sandheap of individuals, all equal and undifferentiated, unrelated except to the State, but an ascending hierarchy of groups, family, school, town, county, union, Church, &c., &c.[24]

It is the first sentence of this quotation that all the pluralists take as their point of departure. Let us look at life before we try to formulate a theory. What Figgis

[24] *Ibid.*, p. 87.

found was not found by all the pluralists. They all found groups, to be sure, but they would not all admit that they found "an ascending hierarchy." But here the point of dispute is one that can be investigated empirically. Is there an ascending hierarchy, or is there not? His critique of the abstract doctrine of sovereignty in favor of a bias toward the facts of life constitutes the major portion of Figgis's contribution to the pluralist movement.

3. Cole:

A PLURALISTIC THEORY OF GUILD SOCIALISM

G. D. H. Cole, originally a Fabian Socialist, felt the need for a more radical program and became a member of the movement for national guilds. According to his theory Cole rejected the doctrine of state sovereignty on the ground that it is not functionally democratic. He rejected as well, and on the same ground, the existing structure of society and the state.

He formulated two principles as to the nature of true democracy. On the basis of these principles he not only rejected the current theory and practice of government but also attempted to outline an organization of society which by its very adherence to those principles would be truly democratic. Also, though this is not the essential point of his argument, however much it was used in making converts, such a society would operate more smoothly and satisfy more needs better than the existing society.

At the bottom of Cole's notion of true democracy and behind both his principles is a view concerning the nature of human personality. Man in society is a complex being, complex especially in his interests and in the groups with which he associates. The aim of a democratic society should be to satisfy men's wants in an orderly system and at the same time to secure their freedom. It is this emphasis on freedom which we recognized as the basic theme in Figgis and which partially verifies our reference to him as a pluralist,[1] which must be considered before Cole's thought can be understood. For Figgis freedom of groups meant noninterference by the state in the internal affairs of groups. From his failure to elaborate the implications of this view we saw that in Figgis's thought it could lead in any one of several directions. Cole made an attempt to be more explicit on this point.

Like Figgis, he advocated freedom of groups from external control on matters of internal policy. For Figgis this was enough, when secure, to produce a free society. Cole saw that this merely posed the problem. First, we must ask the question, what is a group? We have seen the problem involved in Figgis's answer. Cole has more to say on that point. Second, we must consider the grounds for group freedom. Third, we must inquire what kind of organization of control is compatible with the freedom and the purposes of groups.

Two books by Cole, both published in 1920, stand as his attempts to formulate the results of his thought on these matters. A few words about the books themselves are necessary for any attempt to understand his answers. *Social Theory,* published first, is a sociological work which serves as a theoretical formulation of the principles on which rest Cole's rejection of the old state theory and his adherence to functional democracy. In it the attempt is made to come to grips with the old theory and to replace it with a more adequate theory. Taking as his point

[1] *Vide infra* for contrast between Cole and Hobson.

of departure the old theory, he of necessity clings to some of the older terminology, especially in the consideration of the question of the state. *Guild Socialism Restated,* an elaboration of the views which he had previously expressed in a "Fabian Tract" (No. 192), *Guild Socialism,* is written chiefly in terms of economics and makes less effort to adjust itself to previous political thinking. In order to avoid any misunderstanding, the two books must be taken for what they are—the one, theoretical sociology; the other, practical economics.

Society, for Cole, is made up of a multiplicity of associations of various kinds. He defines an association as "any group of persons pursuing a common purpose or aggregation of purposes by a course of coöperative action extending beyond a single act, and, for this purpose laying down, in however rudimentary a form, rules for common action." [2] All associations have two aspects. In relation to the individual they serve to further some interest; in relation to society in general, on the other hand, associations must be considered under the category "function."

Function, as we have seen emerges clearly when, and only when, an association is regarded, not in isolation but in relation to other associations and individuals, that is, to some extent in relation to a system of associations, a Society, and a system of associations and individuals, a community. Such a system implies a more or less clear demarcation of spheres as between the various functional associations in order that each may make its proper contribution to the whole without interfering with the others.[3]

This "contribution to the whole" seems to suggest some underlying common interest.

[2] *Social Theory,* p. 37.   [3] *Ibid.,* p. 55.

Due performance by each association of its social function, on the other hand, not only leads to smooth working and coherence in social organization, but also removes the removable hindrances to the "good life" of the individual. In short, function is the key not only to "social" but to communal and personal well-being.[4]

The influence of Green and Bradley is evident here.

This notion of "function" is basic in Cole's social theory. One aspect of it has been made apparent here, namely, functional organization. That society is best which is organized according to functions. Since there are many associations, for reasons that will be clear below, it is necessary to distinguish two types. In the working of society some associations are essential and others are not. Cole establishes a practical criterion of "essentiality." "The key to essentiality is thus the performance of some function which is vital to the coherent working of society, and without which society would be lopsided or incomplete." [5] The following are the essential associations: political associations—which are concerned with the personal relationships between individuals which arise from the fact that men live together in communities; vocational associations—which in Guild Socialism become the industrial guilds of producers; and appetitive associations—which are organizations of consumers. In Figgis one has the feeling that all associations are essential, but that they have varying degrees of importance.

Given such a preliminary analysis of society and its general structure and principle of organization, for the purposes of this inquiry there are two chief problems: the nature of government and the state and their limits.

[4] *Ibid.*, p. 62.   [5] *Ibid.*, p. 75.

Cole's analysis of the problem of government brings to bear his second basic principle. The only truly democratic government is self-government. In a truly democratic society, the principle of self-government will be put into practice in every group in the community. This attitude, together with the second aspect of the principle of function, namely, functional representation, enables us to explain Cole's views on government. Cole held that no human personality can be represented as a whole and still remain free. Hence the only kind of representation compatible with the principles of democracy is the representation of interests, or, in social terms, functional representation. Functional representation means that each individual has as many representatives as he has interests or partakes in functions. This implies that no man puts his whole personality in any one association. On the basis of these two principles, it is not surprising that there is no general problem of government of the whole community for Cole. For him government is an affair of associations. Each association has its own democratically chosen managerial set-up, or government. The society is democratic when all its associations are democratically self-governing.

Since a consideration of government indicates only the internal structure of associations, we are forced to look to Cole's view of the state as a possible source of information concerning the general organization of society. However, we find no such information. Cole chose to designate the state as that association which deals with those things "which affect all its members more or less equally and the same way." [6] We must notice several things concerning this definition of the state. In the first place, from

[6] *Ibid.*, p. 96.

its general function we can discern an element of continuity with the state of classical theory. In fact, on some such basis as this a theory of state sovereignty can be erected. However, in the second place, we must recognize that for Cole the state is merely an association of individuals with certain common interests. As an association it must be on a par with other associations. Its functions are (1) to represent the interests of men as consumers and (2) to deal with political questions, that is, with questions of personal relationships. It would not do to have one association regulate the relations between other associations. Such a society would violate the principles of functional representation and self-government and hence would not be democratic. Thus we do not find the integrating principle of society in the state. This is Cole's rejection of the theory of the sovereignty of the state. It also serves to differentiate Cole's position from that of Figgis. Cole denies that groups can be free if one group regulates others. However, he gets into the same difficulty of internal versus external actions in another way.

Cole's theory of the state as outlined in the book *Social Theory* is confused, because he was breaking away from the old state theory, but had not yet completely rejected it. This is shown by his simultaneous rejection of the state's sovereignty and his assertion that the state is a compulsory association that can coerce its members. The difficulty here is that by his very definition of the state all men in the community must belong to it. This fact makes the state distinctive—not the fact that it can coerce its members. All associations can do the latter. Cole preserves democracy by insisting that with political rights all men can actively take part in the affairs of the state.

Hence, though it is not voluntary, it is still democratic.

That Cole was not satisfied with this account of the state is evident from his later book, *Guild Socialism Restated*. In that book the state is rejected entirely, and various types of organization of consumers are substituted for it. Hobson's criticism, which cast doubt on the assertion that men have a common interest as consumers, had its effect. How he treats political questions in the new set-up must be considered briefly below.

Since neither government nor the state afforded us any clue as to the integrating technique in society, what Cole refers to as the problem of "coördination," we must look elsewhere. First we must consider who is to regulate the relations between guilds. This is answered simply, and in accordance with the principle of self-government, by the establishment of a Guild Congress made up of representatives of the guilds. The crucial problem is: what body will coördinate the activities of all the Guilds and the state (still considering Cole's first statement of his views) and the individuals. The nature of this coördination must be considered first. It does not mean the determination of the ordinary relations between associations, since those would be determined by a process of negotiation. The problem of coördination arises only when relations between associations become matters of dispute which cannot be negotiated and are outside the sphere of the Guild Congress, that is, concern other bodies besides guilds. It is clear that coördination is in this sense a judicial function. Cole's account of coördination as given in *Social Theory* is stated succinctly in the following quotations:

The co-ordinating body must be not any single association, but a combination of associations, a federal body in which some or all of the various functional associations are linked together.[7]

The co-ordinating agency can only be a combination not of all associations, but of all essential associations, a Joint Council or Congress of the supreme bodies representing each of the main functions in Society. Each functional association will see to the execution of its own function, and for the co-ordination of the activities of the various associations there must be a joint body representative of them.[8]

It does not in the normal case initiate; it decides. It is not so much a legislature as a constitutional judiciary, or democratic Supreme Court of Functional Equity.

This involves that the judiciary and the whole paraphernalia of law and police must be under the control of the co-ordinating body.[9]

In *Guild Socialism Restated,* where Cole has rejected the whole analysis of the state, we have another and more detailed account of the coördinating body. If we consider the case of a single town, we find that all the various associations in it, industrial guilds, coöperatives, collective utilities, civic guilds, cultural and health associations, are represented through their councils in a town commune. This town commune is the local counterpart of the coördinating body mentioned above. In this account, however, the town communes are organized into regional communes, and these latter are organized into a national commune, which is the coördinating body of the whole community. The following quotation indicates its similarity to the coördinating body already described. It differs in that questions of personal relationships will be the business of the local communes.[10]

[7] Page 134. [8] Pages 135–36.
[9] Page 137. [10] See *Guild Socialism Restated,* p. 154.

The national co-ordinating machinery of Guild Society would be essentially unlike the present State, and would have few direct administrative functions. It would be mainly a source of a few fundamental decisions on policy, demarcation between functional bodies, and similar issues, and of final adjudications on appeals in cases of dispute . . . as long as military and naval force continued to be employed, it would have to exercise directly the control of such force, as it would indirectly and in the last resort of the law. Foreign relations, so far as they did not deal exclusively with matters falling within the sphere either of the economic or of the civic bodies, would fall to its lot. . . . Its general structure would thus be essentially the same as that of the smaller Communes which, equally with the national functional bodies, it would exist to co-ordinate. It would be a much less imposing body as the central organ of Society than the Great Leviathan of to-day, with its huge machinery of coercion and bureaucratic government.[11]

With the general picture of Cole's position in mind, we can consider the philosophic assumptions and implications of his effort. Cole attempted to expound a view of society as it should be, as distinguished from society as it is. This implies a criticism of society as it is, which at times becomes explicit. His criticism rests chiefly on moral grounds. Wage slavery and the commodity theory of labor are immoral. He sets the problem in this way: What sort of social organization is implied in the rejection of wage slavery and the commodity theory of labor? The rejection of these implies the rejection of the notion of profits. The immediate concern becomes the necessity of providing a concept of organization to replace profit, that is, to perform the function that profit performs in capitalistic society. The guildsmen and others felt that "function" was a concept on which the organization of

[11] *Ibid.*, pp. 136–37.

society could be more justly based. The wider implications of the idea of function have been, to a certain extent, worked out by Tawney (*The Acquisitive Society*), with regard to the concept of property. In general it may be said that the term implies a realization that a coherent organization of society cannot be founded on rights alone. It marks a return to the idea of duty, but avoids the use of that term because of its moral and theological implications. The term "function" has the advantage that it suggests a working together of the parts of society. It is a secularized and materialistic kind of duty.

The moral attitude at the bottom of Cole's position comes out as well in his rejection of the sovereign state. If we neglect Cole's analysis of the state in *Social Theory*, since he himself rejected it in his later formulation, we find the following considerations on the subject in *Guild Socialism Restated*.

We have so far attacked the notion of universal State Sovereignty from two distinct points of view, and have, I think, made large breaches in the theory, without as yet destroying it altogether. First, we criticised the structure of the State from the point of view of functional democracy, showing that its undifferentiated representative theory unfitted it to be the expression of a democratic spirit which ought to find utterance in every separate aspect of social activity. By this criticism we destroyed the idea of State "omnicompetence." Secondly, in dealing with Collectivist theories in the economic sphere, we destroyed the idea that the State represents the consumer, and so excluded it from functional participation in the control of industry or service.[12]

After making these criticisms, he still feels that he has to come to grips with a revised view of a state "whose function is Sovereignty." [13] This is the view that the state

[12] Pages 119–20.   [13] *Ibid.*, p. 120.

is merely the coördinating body in society. He argues as follows:

> But it may be argued that the defence of the State, in its new form, meets this argument; for the new "function of the State" is simply co-ordination and nothing else. This contention, however, will not hold water; for the co-ordination of functions is not, and cannot be, itself a function. Either co-ordination includes the functions which it co-ordinates, in which case the whole of social organization comes again under the domination of the State, and the whole principle of functional democracy is destroyed; or it excludes them, and in this case it clearly cannot co-ordinate. In other words, the State "representative" either controls the economic and civic spheres, or he does not: if he does, the representatives in these spheres lose their self-government; if he does not, he cannot regulate their mutual relationships.[14]
>
> We have then, to seek a new form of co-ordinating body which will not be inconsistent with the functional democracy on which our whole system is based. This can be nothing other than a bringing together of the various functional bodies whose separate working we have already described. Co-ordination is inevitably coercive unless it is self-co-ordination, and it must therefore be accomplished by the common action of the various bodies, which require co-ordination.[15]

Although, as we have seen, Cole realizes the necessity of coercion in the last analysis,[16] he aims, by means of the structure which he gives to the coördinating body, to reduce it to a minimum.

Cole's analysis of freedom has been suggested. His thesis is that a man is free so long as he has a different representative for each of his interests and has certain rights of recall. The point of this is that if one man represents you for all your interests, some of his views may not coincide with yours, and on these points you will not be

[14] Ibid., pp. 122–23.   [15] Ibid., p. 124.   [16] Ibid., p. 156.

represented in the body that makes decisions; you will not be self-governing, and hence not free. The attempt to achieve freedom by devolution, which is characteristic of most of the pluralists, must be understood, not as an attempt at absolute freedom, which they realized was impossible, but at freedom from some central irresponsible body. Cole's version of this is to limit each body in society to one function and to make them all responsible to the bodies or individuals which they represent.

It is characteristic of all the pluralists, also, that they make their analyses in social terms rather than in merely political terms. Cole broadens the basis of the discussion by bringing in the economic societies, just as Figgis brought in the religious ones. He makes the now familiar assertion that political democracy is impossible without economic democracy and, as I have shown, makes the latter quite clear. What does become a mystery, however, is the nature of the "political." Political activities, according to Cole, are those which affect all men in a like manner. If we look at his work as a whole, this comes down, in the end, to the regulation of matters of personal relationships. We are in the habit of calling this "private law," but why call it political?

The most common criticism of Cole's position, indeed of Guild Socialism in general, is that it multiplies groups to bewildering complexity and produces an unwieldy social organization. Since Cole does not say which associations will be provided for in the constitution of the guild state, and since he does not say how new groups are to be added, although he insists that provision for such addition must be made, we must accept his view that groups will be organized as they become necessary. However, any observer of the history of societies would say that happens without Guild Socialism.

Finally, there is the question of public policy. Like the Constitution of the United States, Cole's version of Guild Socialism makes no provision for the existence and operation of political parties. For those who see the existence of a plurality of political parties as the basis of democracy Cole's society may not seem democratic. Yet, for Cole political parties, since they are not based on functional representation, are not democratic.

In summary, the aim of Cole's whole theory is an attempt to organize functionally the expression and just reconciliation of all possible group interests. By taking the interests of all groups into consideration, any unity in society will be an achieved unity rather than a formal *a priori* unity. In view of this, Cole can accurately be said to express the pluralistic attitude.

As a result of Cole's analysis several problems come to light which must be noted because they not only show the difficulties into which Cole's theory is driven but also because they exhibit issues fundamental to any pluralistic approach to political theory. These issues will be stated at this point. The consideration of a possible method of solving them will be reserved for the last chapter.

Cole distinguishes two types of social control: governmental control and coördination. Governmental control is concerned with the promotion of interests or functions. Individuals having a common interest or participating in a given function elect representatives to administer the function in their interest. Government or, as Cole would have it, self-government arises only with regard to interests or functions. That it is not possible to analyze social activity solely in terms of interests and functions is indicated by the necessity of the other form of control, namely, coördination. Everything social that cannot be called a function comes, for Cole, under that branch of control known as coördination. Chief among these is the problem of relations, that is, the adjustments of the interests of groups. Coördination is the process of democratically or mutually adjusting relations, whether they are between individuals or between groups, or between individuals and groups. Second among those things that seem to be dealt with under coördination in the commune set-up are problems of geography. Cole seems to hesitate to admit geographic considerations, but when he does, it is to the commune that he gives the function of regulating matters arising from the geographic nature of the community. Although in some cases Cole does not seem to make quite clear whether a given matter comes under a functional association or under the coördinating body, as a general rule it may be said that for him everything that is the result of a general and enduring interest is a function, while everything else, when in need of control or settlement, comes under the coördinating body.

The conclusion that we can draw from this, that there is no general interest in coördination on the part of any definable group in the community, or, as Cole puts it, that coördination is not a function, is worthy of consideration. If the common good, or "contribution to the whole," as Cole puts it in one place,[17] is the aim of all social organization, we may suppose that the interest in coördination is the supreme interest of all men in society. But Cole does not hold this view: the desire for freedom wins out. Hence the problem of coördination arises for

[17] *Social Theory,* p. 55.

him, not as a general situation which concerns all men at all times, but as a series of particular problems concerning merely those men or interests which come into conflict. If coördination can be called an interest at all for Cole, it is not a true interest, since it is a temporary one that disappears once the particular conflict that gives rise to it has been settled. The problems that arise from this discussion are: (1) How far can society be considered merely as the organization of interests? (2) If it cannot be described adequately in this way, what other factors must be considered? (3) What is the relation of government or administration to what Cole calls coördination? (4) Can there be said to be a general interest in, or a general problem of, coördination?

That Guild Socialism is not necessarily pluralistic and that its pluralism appears only in Cole's version of it can be shown by a brief account of the views of the other chief protagonist of the movement who elaborated a political theory, namely, S. G. Hobson.

In *National Guilds and the State* Hobson distinguishes man as a member of any association from man as "citizen."

In any event, when I come to consider the case of the producer as such, I shall contend that as between him and the consumer his must be the final word; whilst as between the producer and the citizen, the citizen must decide and speak the final word through the State. The State, whatever its ultimate form, must be the expression of the life of the citizen community.[18]

We are obviously led to seek for an elaboration of the phrase "life of the citizen community." We can find other expressions for the same notion. The state comes

[18] *Op. cit.*, p. 32.

in only in cases of "public policy." It protects "citizen rights." We find further that the state is an organ of last resort.[19] If we attempt to ask what is the function of the state (a concrete question), we find that the state expresses the general will of the citizens, which amounts to saying that the state, though sovereign, has no particular function. In order to keep the state sovereign and yet to get administrative functions performed, Hobson introduces government as a separate organ. He says, "My own concepts rather lead me to the conclusion that the government, in all its ramifications, derives its authority from and must ultimately have its functions defined by, the State, which I regard as the organized expression of citizenship, the sovereign authority." [20] Hobson believes that it is possible to have a body representative of the whole of all the people; Cole does not. Cole is a pluralist; Hobson, in the last analysis, is not.[21] For Hobson [22] all power and authority are at the top and are distributed to associations which exist only with the consent of the state.

The general problem that arises from this comparison of the views of the Guild Socialists is that of the relation of pluralistic political theory to proposals for innovations in the organization or the administration of the state or the government. From the comparison made here, it is apparent that pluralism is more than a mere change in the institutional organization of a given society.

[19] *Ibid.*, p. 61.   [20] *Ibid.*, p. 101.

[21] Willoughby (*The Ethical Basis of Political Authority*, p. 443) suggests that Hobson is not a pluralist, but he fails to elaborate the point clearly.

[22] *National Guilds and the State*, p. 127.

4. Laski:

INDIVIDUALISTIC PLURALISM

We may in general discern several positions in the development of Laski's political thought. These positions are not necessarily to be taken as conflicting with one another. They are rather shifts of emphasis brought about chiefly by changes in the current political situation and by the new ideas with which he came into contact. In considering Laski's theory it is important to have constantly in mind the fact that he is and has been a member of the British Labour Party. With that before one, many changes in position and emphasis become clear which otherwise might be unintelligible. Thus, we might distinguish the inner and the outer dynamic of Laski's position. The outer has been referred to and may in the course of the discussion be used to account for the otherwise unaccountable. The inner dynamic is the chief subject of this essay.

The problems of political theory, for Laski, are focused on a critique of the concept of sovereignty, which implies a moral criticism of the idea of command.[1] In his first book, *The Problem of Sovereignty,* this critique takes the form of an attack on the theory which holds that the state is absolute. According to this theory the state's actions consist of commands, and these commands have to

[1] *Foundations of Sovereignty,* p. 245.

be obeyed on moral, legal, and prudential grounds. The disobedience of these commands implies a negation of the state. To an idealist whose theory of the moral life was developed in terms of self-realization it was difficult to explain how an act of obedience could be an act of self-realization. T. H. Green had admitted it in fact, though he conceded it to be a paradox. Bosanquet had begged the question by assuming it and asserting it vigorously.

Laski criticizes this doctrine on three grounds: (1) It makes impossible the moral judgment on the part of individuals of particular acts of the state. If the state is one, it must be judged as a whole. Its acts cannot be judged individually. The implication is that this view makes impossible man's acting as an independent moral agent, for such action implies a judgment of what is right and action on that judgment. If the state is identical with morality and is one, whatever is in the state is right, and self-realization is possible in the state and only there. (2) This doctrine does not square with the facts as we know them. There never was, that is, a state which had the monopoly on self-realization which the monistic theory claims as the essence of statehood. States are sometimes obeyed and sometimes not. There are practical limits to what the state can demand of its members. (3) There exist other organizations in human society which also have a certain claim on men and which cannot be said to owe their existence to the state.[2]

To correct the theory of the state, Laski, in effect enun-

[2] "The advocates of pluralism are convinced that this [monistic state] is both administratively incomplete and ethically inadequate."—*Ibid.*, p. 240.

ciates three propositions: (1) The state is one association among others, competing with them for support. (2) Sovereignty is the ability to secure consent. (3) It is the nature of man as a moral being to judge the actions of the state and to support those which he deems right. This is the basis of Laski's pluralistic theory of the state.

In spite of these criticisms, Laski's position still depended largely on ideas derived from the idealists. It is important to see what he accepted, consciously or unconsciously. The notion of the state as something to be obeyed is retained, but the state is deprived of its aura of holiness and demoted to a position of competition with other groups. The concept of sovereignty is retained, but it is redefined so that it ceases to be anything but a name for the ability to secure obedience.[3] In other words, we still have a state, it still issues commands, and, if the commands are obeyed, it is still sovereign. The two things that are in doubt are whether the state or some other group will command and whether the commands will be obeyed. Though the state continues to be moral, its acts, not the state as a whole, are to be judged.

Once the state is relegated to a fluctuating position among other associations, the burden of Laski's insight rests on the awareness that it is unrealistic to say *a priori* that the state's actions are going to be right [4] and will be obeyed.[5] That only time can tell. And if the state does something wrong (something that a large group holds to

[3] In other places, especially in his later works, Laski goes back to the old way of speaking of sovereignty. This is especially true in his legal writings. See *Studies in Law and Politics*, p. 237.

[4] *Grammar of Politics*, p. 28.

[5] *Foundations of Sovereignty*, p. 245. Here Laski puts the acts of the state on a moral parity with those of other associations.

be wrong), it will not be obeyed,[6] but nevertheless the state will continue to exist in view of the continuance of obedience to its right acts. For Laski the problem is solved when sovereignty is squared with the notion of democracy by transforming consent to the state as a whole into a *seriatim* consent to particular acts. Bosanquet solved the problem by making a farce of the notion of consent. Laski performs the same operation on the notion of sovereignty. Sovereignty is plural for two reasons: now one group, then another, may be obeyed; and, secondly, one act may be obeyed and another of the same group disobeyed. Sovereignty is no longer the essence of the state, but merely the measure of consent. This pluralistic theory was realistic not merely from the point of view of the facts of consent but from the point of view of the law as well, because many of the states at that time admitted that citizens could sue the government.

Having disposed of sovereignty as a peculiar attribute of the state, Laski is forced to turn his attention to its instrument, government. It is government through which the state acts, and since we are interested in practical political actions, it is at government that we must look.[7] Even though no state possesses sovereignty as Austin defined it, yet we cannot deny, as a matter of fact, that acts of government do have a certain "authority." Governments have power, but power alone does not constitute authority. Nor is the legal authority with which courts deal what Laski has in mind. He is concerned with what we can call the "moral authority of government," that is, the claim to obedience which the acts of government

---

[6] *Grammar of Politics*, p. 284.
[7] *Foundations of Sovereignty*, p. 27; *Grammar of Politics*, p. 28; *Authority in the Modern State*, p. 30.

LASKI: INDIVIDUALISTIC PLURALISM

have on man as a moral being. The problems to be dealt with are: What is the nature of this authority of government in the modern state? What is its relation to the authority of other groups (if there be such authority)? And finally, how ought the individual to view this authority?

In order to understand how power, neutral in itself, is transformed into authority,[8] we must consider the end of the state. Just what is the end of the state, according to Laski, is no clear matter in his early books.[9] However, that the state has an end [10] there can be no doubt, and that is what is relevant here. Presumably this end is stated and fully known to all citizens. The point is that the state, in theory or in practice, is not to be judged on the basis of its aim, even its stated aim. That is merely the frame of reference. The state as such is not to be judged at all. Assuming that the end of the state is known, it is the individual actions of government that are to be judged by individual citizens in the frame of reference of the aims of the state. This elaboration of the view presented in his earlier writings brings to light certain new elements in Laski's view of the state. Sovereignty, taken from the state, is now attributed to the state-purpose.[11] Although individual acts of the state are to be criticized

---

[8] *Grammar of Politics*, p. 36.

[9] *Ibid.*, p. 40. Here Laski suggests that the aim of the state is to achieve the common good. "I am entitled to examine the State upon the hypothesis that its will is directed to ends other than the common good."

[10] *Foundations of Sovereignty*, p. 62. It is suggested that the purpose is discovered from an investigation of actual processes. See also *Authority in the Modern State*, p. 61.

[11] *Authority in the Modern State*, p. 53. "Our ultimate allegiance is always to the ideal."—*Grammar of Politics*, p. 27. "A government, I have argued, is limited by the purpose that it serves."—*Ibid.*, p. 134. This view reaches clarity in *The State in Theory and Practice* (p. 41) and *Studies in Law and Politics* (p. 246).

in the light of this general purpose of the state, no indication is given that the purpose of the state itself is subject to criticism.

This view is a result of the awareness on the part of Laski that power can be and is used for selfish purposes. That governments do not constantly and consistently carry out the state's purposes, but rather tend to carry out the aims of those in control of government (usually the economically powerful), is the reason why power is not authoritative simply because it is in the hands of government. What is needed is some objective reference by means of which to test the results of the use of power. The avowed aim of the state provides this reference. While this device prevents the perversion of power in the first instance, the judgment of the rightness and the wrongness of governmental acts in the light of an end creates difficulties of its own. In effect it does not escape from the difficulty of all idealistic thinking about politics, namely, that once we have postulated an end, the rationalization of even apparently incongruous ends is possible. Assuming good faith on the part of the judges of governmental acts, we must realize further that the criticism of these acts is a technical matter requiring technical skill and training which most individual citizens do not possess. Laski realizes this and sees also that one of the central problems of his whole theory is to combine the advantages of technical training with the individual judgment of governmental acts which he considers essential to democracy. He attempts to solve this problem by insisting that in every case the findings of all experts be made known, but the decision should remain, in the last analysis, with the conscience of the individual citizen.

Thus far what we have is an idealistic theory, reminiscent of Green's, for although the state-purpose is not clearly indicated, it seems to consist, from the indications given, in maintaining the conditions of the good life.[12] The differences, aside from those of language, are not significant. Instead of the state, the state-purpose is sovereign. But in the crucial case of the suspected perversion of state power this is what Green himself believed when he admitted the propriety of resistance to the state.[13] Green's problem was to explain how an act of obedience can be a moral act of self-realization—as he asserted it to be. Laski solved this by showing that acts of obedience are acts of consent. The state has authority, not by virtue of its purpose, but by virtue of the acts that it performs to attain that purpose.[14] Both insist that self-realization is a matter of the individual and that all institutions, including government, are means. It remains to be seen how much the emphatic discussions of pluralism alter this picture of the resemblance between the theories of the two men, since Green never claimed to be a pluralist.

The idealistic notions inherent in Laski's theory of the state, the emphasis on oneness found therein, exhibit merely one aspect of his position. The unity of the state mentioned above is only a unity of purpose. This unity

---

[12] "It aims at the development of the fullest capacity for good possessed by its members."—*Foundations of Sovereignty*, p. 88. See also *Authority in the Modern State*, p. 41; and *Grammar of Politics*, p. 39.

[13] "The general principle that the citizen must never act otherwise than as a citizen, does not carry with it an obligation under all conditions to conform to the law of his state, since those laws may be inconsistent with the true end of the state as the sustainer and harmonizer of social relations."—*Principles of Political Obligation*, p. 148.

[14] *Grammar of Politics*, pp. 26–27, 36, 286. In the last-cited quotation he applies this position to the nature of law.

of purpose, to be sure, goes far beyond the state. Laski conceived of a unity of the social purpose as well.[15] His pluralism consists in the recognition of the claim to sovereignty of other groups besides the state and in his insistence on the real personality of these other groups.[16] However, what distinguishes these other groups, besides their personnel, is not their aims. These are identical with the state's. For Laski all groups try to establish the conditions of the good life. It is the means chosen that distinguish the state from the church and from the trade union. Laski sees these groups as competing with each other.[17] Each tries to convince the public that its way is the most satisfactory one to reach the top of the hill.[18] This view is in sharp distinction to the idealistic view of Bosanquet and to the view of Hobhouse. It is also to be distinguished from the doctrine of real personality as elaborated by Figgis and from the ultimate aim of Guild Socialism. These views insist that all these various groups must coöperate to attain the common good. Laski rejected this view because it destroyed freedom. The individual moral being had no voice as to how the social good was to be attained in the idealistic theories. It was determined *a priori,* in the case of Bosanquet, that all groups formed an organic whole. In the case of Hobhouse the continuous growth in the harmony between groups was an irresistible historical process. We have the feeling that Figgis leaned toward the organic theory of Gierke on this point. For Cole the aim of all social organization is to establish one harmonious machine for the produc-

[15] *Foundations of Sovereignty,* p. 219; *Grammar of Politics,* p. 25.
[16] *Foundations of Sovereignty,* pp. 67–68.
[17] *Ibid.,* pp. 170–71. This might be said to be an expression of the extreme of radical pluralism, where it merges with anarchism.
[18] *Problem of Sovereignty,* p. 285.

tion of goods. Laski feels that there may be harmony, but there may not; and that we cannot presuppose it.[19] If we turn to history, he says, we find that the evidence is against the existence of such harmony. That the state is an organic unity identifiable with society he denies completely. Oneness is the way of subjection. He is concerned for freedom.[20] His problem is to combine the maximum of freedom with the achievement of the state's purpose. His account of the concept of rights enables him to do this.

If we conceive of the state-purpose as beginning as a vague notion and gradually in the course of history becoming clearer and clearer, we shall not find it difficult to realize that in the course of this development certain things were found to be essential to the attainment of that end. The recognition of those things on the part of the state and the guaranteeing of them to the citizens is the establishment of rights.[21] They are analogous to the rules of a game. They limit what you may do, but without them you could not play or win at all. Laski considers these rights, in his early works, chiefly as a limitation on the state.[22]

[19] In *Foundations of Sovereignty* (p. 76) he takes a more extreme position and suggests that any ultimate harmony, for example, between capital and labor, seems impossible under present conditions.

[20] *Ibid.*, pp. 86–87. "The real truth is that the members of the State are powerless against an efficient centralization wielded in the interest of any social fragment, however large. It prevents the balance of associations which is the safeguard of liberty . . . the secret of liberty is the division of power. But that political system in which the division of power is most securely maintained is a federal system, and, indeed, there is a close connection between the idea of federalism and the idea of liberty."

[21] These rights are natural both in that the state-purpose cannot be fulfilled without them and in that they do not depend on the state for their validity.—*Foundations of Sovereignty*, p. 246; *Grammar of Politics*, pp. 40, 91 f.

[22] *Grammar of Politics*, p. 104.

This analysis provides the answers to the problems set. Power becomes authoritative when it recognizes its two limitations: (1) It must act in accordance with the state-purpose. (2) It must recognize rights.[23] These are the two aspects of the subjection of the state to its purpose.[24] The violation of the second is *prima facie* evidence of the violation of the first. It is the individual who judges.

In considering Laski's later writings the problem is to see what happened to his pluralism and why. If we go back and ask what it was that was plural in his earlier work, we find two main lines of thought. In the first place, the groups that had to be taken into account by the political theorist were plural. There were other groups besides the state, and they were significant for both the self-realization of individuals and the purposes of the political analyst. Secondly, and deriving from this plurality of political groups, is the pluralism of sovereignty. Once Laski had reduced sovereignty to mere ability to secure consent, all groups that had that ability and every group insofar as it had that ability could be said to be sovereign.

This analysis *seems* to be wholly rejected in Laski's *The State in Theory and Practice*. Sovereignty is once again, as in the idealistic thinkers, the peculiar attribute of the state. There is no talk of the plurality of groups. We have what amounts to a duality of groups, now called "classes" in accordance with the Marxist analysis, which Laski took over in large part.

[23] *Ibid.*, p. 105.
[24] The analysis of pluralism in its two aspects (note 2, above) suggests an analogous analysis of power which can be seen in *Grammar of Politics* (pp. 36, 38–39). Power has two aspects: (1) It is morally neutral; hence it requires scrutiny on the part of the individual in the light of the state-purpose to give it moral validity. (2) Administratively it lends itself to use for selfish ends; hence individuals need rights.

LASKI: INDIVIDUALISTIC PLURALISM

If we compare the early and the later views, we find that Laski went from the position that sovereignty had to be justified by its acts to the position that if the right group, the workers, gained control of the force at the disposal of the state, the necessary social reforms (the program of the Labour Party) would follow. The latter position results from a problem of practical politics. The problem of political theory is: how is the existence of the state compatible with the moral self-realization of individuals? The solution is that we should obey the state only in those cases in which we morally approve of its actions. In this way obedience implies consent, and consent implies self-realization. The problem of action, on the other hand, is to ascertain how certain desirable reforms can be achieved. The answer is, by having the workers obtain control of the state. In the first situation Laski acts the part of a political philosopher, and in that role he discerns the existence of a plurality of groups. Regarding the latter situation he writes as a member of one of those groups, namely, the working class, or rather the British Labour Party, and in that role he became aware of and pointed out the difficulties that the Labour Party would have in attempting to attain power.[25]

Government by consent is an aim or an ideal. It is the ideal of democracy in the sense that we will not have true democracy until force is eliminated and things are done by consent. Thus consent becomes the measure of democracy.

In analyzing the existing political situation Laski finds that relationships and political activity are determined by one group in society, the economically powerful. His problem, on the basis of this analysis, is to show how this

[25] *Parliamentary Government in England, passim.*

condition can be transformed into one in which governmental activity is determined by the consent of the whole people or as large a part of the whole as is feasible. How, he must ask, can the power of the economically strong be diminished and that of the rest of the population be increased so that government by consent of all the governed has some possibility of realization?

One of the principles which Laski took over from Marxism is that no powerful group will give up its power voluntarily. When it sees its position menaced, it fights. Thus those who oppose such a group must also be prepared to fight. The question is how Laski got to this position from his earlier view. We must reconsider his earlier view in the light of this analysis.

In his early writings the powerful group which dominated society and which had to be curbed was the state. This was the period of anti-state feeling. It was felt that the state claimed more power than was its rightful share. The weapon to oppose this power, that is, the theoretical weapon, was political pluralism, the insistence on the real personality of other groups besides the state and the assertion that these groups must be considered as ultimate in their respective spheres.

In the development of his thought Laski found that the state was a nebulous affair; and when he tried to make it concrete, he found that its essential element was force, military or police. In examining the working of society he also found that this force was in the hands of the economically powerful. He then realized that to oppose the state was not enough. It was more important to oppose those who controlled the active power of the state, the capitalist class. This class becomes the enemy of government by consent because it controls government in its own interest. Laski shifts from the view that history shows that no group can be sovereign (omnicompetent) to the view that one group is as a matter of fact effectively sovereign. He claims for the capitalist class what he denied to the state. The insistence on the real personality and ultimate significance of other groups becomes of importance only for the more distant future. The immediate need is for the overthrow of the small controlling group by some other larger and more inclusive group that can more truly represent the people as a whole, so that eventually the people can provide their own representation. That larger group is the workers, represented in England by the Labour Party.

All this is not to assert that the ultimate aim is not the same. It is only the result of the awareness on the part of Laski that the immediate problem is more difficult than he had anticipated and requires a different analysis.

A further comment on the shift in Laski's emphasis is provided by some of his more recent writings. He wrote recently:

Federalism, I suggest, is the appropriate governmental technique for an expanding capitalism, in which the price of local habit—which means, also, delay—admits compensation in the total outcome. But a contracting capitalism cannot afford the luxury of federalism. It is insufficiently positive in character; it does not provide for sufficient rapidity of action; it inhibits the emergence of necessary standards of uniformity; it relies upon compacts and compromises which take insufficient account of the category of time; it leaves the backward areas a restraint, at once parasitic and poisonous, on those who seek to move forward; not least, its psychological results, especially in an age of crisis are depressing to a democracy that needs the drama of positive achievement to retain its faith.[26]

At present the motivating forces of Laski's thought are the need for action, positive action, and the need for speed in that action. The problem of freedom and the moral status of the individual in the state are not of special interest now. As a member of a progressive political party, Laski has a program to put forward. The sooner that program is put into action, the better. Freedom can wait until the urgent program of reform is on its way.

It is not difficult to explain this shift in perspective if we turn to what I have called the "outer dynamic" of his thought. His first writing was done during and after the first World War, when it was thought that a new world was in the process of being built. The hopes of the liberals were high. As the twenties dwindled away, with little or no progress in putting into practice the liberal program, his attitude changed. In the thirties, when the collapse of the economic system became apparent, the problems to be dealt with were material ones—the organization of the production and the distribution of goods and services to bring back order and prosperity. For Laski freedom and the moral status of the individual, like federalism, were luxuries that a period of the constriction of capitalism and the rise of fascism made too costly. The emphasis on speed and uniformity in the above quotation show the fear that unless democratic states do something to validate their theory immediately, all will be lost.

Though Laski is fully aware that the balance of power

---

[26] "The Obsolescence of Federalism," *New Republic*, XCVIII, No. 1274 (May 3, 1939), 367.

is invariably in favor of the *status quo*,[27] he is cheered by the fact that in England the Labour Party, one of whose avowed aims is to overthrow the economic system of capitalism, is accepted as the official opposition party. "Granted the nature of the party system, the Opposition will one day become a government." [28] Even then there will be difficulties in introducing the labour program. Laski still maintains the hope that in the long run the parliamentary party system of government will be able to survive the crisis of the transformation of the economic system.[29]

We now come to consider the relevance of the development of Laski's political theory, especially the last phase of this development, to a pluralistic analysis of freedom. In tracing Laski's views we can once again verify the close relationship between pluralism and freedom. Pluralism faded from Laski's thought when the problem of freedom was no longer uppermost in his mind. But it is important to go back and consider carefully what kind of pluralism Laski developed.

Although Laski, following Figgis, insisted on the real personality of groups, he took a great deal from Cole as well. Both Cole and Laski base their pluralism on an idea of human personality. For Cole, we saw, a man develops his personality in various associations, and the functional organization of society and the functional representation of men and societies are the only methods of social organization which preserve and foster human personality. Laski had a different idea of human personality. Basically man is an autonomous moral agent. Any adequate organ-

[27] *Parliamentary Government in England*, pp. 15–16 *et passim*.
[28] *Ibid.*, p. 13.   [29] *Ibid.*, pp. 155–56.

ization of society must be based on that fact. Since man is morally autonomous, he can determine in what his self-realization consists, that is, each man can choose his own ends. The condition that society has to put up with is one in which different men pursue different ends differently.[30] Associations grow out of this pursuit of ends, and hence they are important; but Laski maintains his connection with the old liberalism and distinguishes himself from Cole by insisting that not only does no single association absorb the whole of human personality but also that all associations together cannot. The technological and social changes that make some form of collectivism inevitable shook Laski's pluralism to its foundation. He had to give up his basic premise, which he himself admitted tended toward anarchism, the absolute moral independence of the individual. In the Marxist phase of Laski's thought, we find the individual subordinated to the class, and individual self-realization is pushed into the background by the inevitability of the class struggle.

In recent years, it was suggested above, Laski's thought has taken another shift. This shift back toward parliamentarism was in theory the result of two conflicting strains, both resulting from the challenge of fascism, an undesirable form of collectivism. One was the necessity of validating the efficiency of democracy in the face of fascism; the other was the recognition that fascism is a challenge to freedom and that democracy, to validate itself, must preserve freedom as an integral feature of its social organization.

[30] *Introduction to Politics*, p. 47.

5.

CONCLUSION

The history of political pluralism shows that it has been connected, in both its negative and its positive aspects, with various plans of action. Although some thinkers, for example, Laski, suggest that we will find pluralism in any state and therefore merely plead for the recognition of an existent fact or tendency, other pluralists, for example, Cole, suggest that as a matter of fact society is becoming monistic. Cole argues that in order to safeguard freedom and to insure justice we must establish pluralism. This type of argumentation, from certain principles to an ideal pluralistic society, is doubtless a form of pluralism and has been regarded as such. But, as has been indicated earlier, it is not in plans of action that we find the significance of political pluralism for political theory; that is, such plans of action are not necessarily based on pluralistic political theory. The failure of the Guild Socialists and the mutations of Laski's political thought indicate, among other things, that pluralism is not a satisfactory fighting philosophy for those whose aim is to make society over all at once and on a grand scale.[1] By its very nature, pluralism does not

[1] Guild Socialism, as a propagandist movement, became monistic, as did Laski, when it entered into the arena of political strife.

CONCLUSION

point to any all-embracing end that can be used to rally the people. On the contrary, it has always been the task of the pluralists to emphasize the distinctness of interests and the separate ways of different people. Monism, on the other hand, with its emphasis on unity, has served admirably as a philosophic foundation for all sorts of political causes. Although a pluralistic analysis of society may be closer to the facts of political life, it is much farther from the principles of mass manipulation than is monism. No matter how pluralistic an analysis of society we may begin with, when we come to do something, we must focus on one object—one basic factor on which we can operate or one enemy who must be crushed. When translated into philosophies of action, the factors that may have been analyzed pluralistically tend to converge. Saying this is not to deny that the analyses of pluralistic political theory do have a certain relevance to the problems of action. What this relevance is will be considered below. Aside from the methods which plans of action tend to follow, there is also the problem of the nature of the plan itself. We can readily see in what sense a plan whose aim is to establish a functional social organization is said to be pluralistic. However, it is one of the tasks of this essay to show that none of these technical forms of social organization is essentially connected with pluralistic social theory. This theory is at once something more, since it is concerned with more than mere organizations, and something less, since it does not indicate any definite plan of action.

After these introductory remarks it becomes possible to restate the aims of pluralistic theory. Taking its clue from political science, rather than from a statement of

CONCLUSION

what ought to be, it attempts to criticize traditional state-theory in the light of recent developments in sociological and economic, as well as political, fact and thought; and in this way it attempts to arrive at a method by which an intelligible analysis of freedom can be carried out. As a result, pluralistic theory makes clear the function and nature of politics, in relation to nonpolitical forms of freedom.

Pluralism, historically, has been a philosophy of freedom. In philosophy proper it has been an attempt to escape from the confines of narrow and rigid systems. In political philosophy it has been an attempt, however unsuccessful, to escape from the organic state theories and to formulate the fundamental content of freedom and democracy.

My discussion will center mainly on the ways in which individuals and groups control the operations of their government, because it is here that political freedom exists. In paying his taxes or obeying the law the citizen is regulated rather than free. In this sense freedom means either freedom from regulation or freedom to regulate. This is irrelevant to the problem of moral freedom as formulated by the idealists.

If we begin by asking what aspects of social organization have been referred to as political, we find that a wide variety of answers are possible, depending on where we go for our information. In the city states of Greece the whole of a free man's life was in the *polis* and in this sense was political. In late eighteenth- and early nineteenth-century England the major aspects of living and working were extra-political. Most other cases rest somewhere between these two extremes. It is not the business

CONCLUSION

of the political theorist to say what the essential nature of "the political" is for all time.[2] The traditional theory of the state starts with general principles and attempts to determine what the nature of the state and political activity must be. It says, in order to have a state, you must have a unified body of citizens. It then raises the question as to the basis of unity. Before inquiring whether there is unity and to what degree, the classical political philosophers, assuming both the necessity for unity and its existence in all true states, raise the question as to how it can be justified. Thus we have the myth of the social contract which establishes the unitary body politic. It is discovered that a unified body politic must have one ultimate source of law; thus the concept of sovereignty arises. The aim is not to discover who or what is or are the governors and over what. Since there must be a sovereign, the aim is rather to justify sovereignty, to show that the loss of freedom it implies is either imaginary[3] or bears more important fruit in justice and peace.[4]

Historically the theoretical interest in the problem of sovereignty ran parallel to the growth of the national

---

[2] Barker writes in defense of the idealistic notion of political theory: "Political theory, like ethical theory, is concerned with what may be called the 'pure' instance—with the conscience of the good man and the 'general will' of the right State. It assumes that the best is the truest, and that the truest is the proper subject of study. Politics and ethics are alike concerned with man at his highest power, and not at his lowest; 'for the real nature of a thing is what the thing is when its growth is fully developed.' There will always be some who will use the lower as the criterion of the higher; there will always be others—and they are not necessarily mistaken—who will use the higher as the criterion of the lower. In any case the idealist does not stand alone in making the ideal the subject of study. Sidgwick was a Utilitarian; but Sidgwick holds that the study of politics 'is concerned primarily with . . . the system of relations which *ought to be* established . . . in a society of civilized men.'"
—*Political Thought from Spencer to Today*, pp. 80–81.

[3] Rousseau, *Social Contract*.   [4] Hobbes, *Leviathan,* chap. xvii.

CONCLUSION

states. The desire for an adequate theory of sovereignty was a result of the need for some theoretical grounds to justify unity. Thus the theories of sovereignty were theories of unity. The elaboration of the bases of sovereignty were indications of the existence of or the need for unity. They were justifications of the state.

Whenever it can be shown that these grounds of sovereignty—social contract, the general will, the common good—become dubious in fact, such change will not merely serve to weaken the doctrine of sovereignty insofar as these are its foundations, but also, which is more important, it will make necessary a reconsideration of the foundations of the state in the absence of such unity.

The doctrine of the sovereignty of the people was the traditional solution for the problem of freedom. The mass of contradictions and irrelevancies that develops from this way of proceeding has led the pluralists and other recent political theorists to go the other way around. By starting with what we see and do, checking what we conclude to be basic by what we see and do, we can be more certain that our theory will have relevance to "facts," that our problems will be real ones and our conclusions verifiable.

With this method in mind the political pluralists found that many of the standard answers to the standard questions of political theory have to be discarded. The attack was focused on the doctrine of sovereignty, especially the doctrine of absolute sovereignty according to Austin. Although the general method was satisfactory, this particular procedure was unfortunate for two reasons. In the first place, as the critics [5] of the pluralists have pointed out, this doctrine of sovereignty was rarely held

[5] Coker and Ellis.

CONCLUSION

in the unqualified manner that some of the pluralists seem to suppose. It was qualified either by moral law or by practical necessity. It reached its peak in the development of the pure theory of law, which is pure because it simply works out the implications of the legal concepts and has nothing to do with any particular state. Secondly, it was not sovereignty that was at the root of the difficulty. It was the concepts of general will, social contract, and common good that furnished grounds for the doctrine of sovereignty. It is to these that the pluralists should have turned their attention. Instead, they (for example, Figgis and Laski) showed that if we look at the history of various states we find that, when crucial situations arose, the state could not validate its claim to sovereignty, it had to give in to other groups. That this had a salutary effect and forced revisers of the theory of sovereignty to take these groups into consideration—to state their qualifications more accurately—cannot be denied. But, unfortunately, the pluralists did not go far enough. For example, although he decentralized sovereignty by distributing it potentially to all small groups, Laski still conceived political theory in terms of the problem of sovereignty, that is, in terms of the means for obtaining consent. One of the purposes of this essay is to show that only by criticizing the more fundamental concepts of the general will and the common good can the political pluralists hope to reduce the doctrine of sovereignty to its proper proportion.

The first question the pluralist should ask is this: Is there, *in fact,* a common good or a general will? If we look at the ways in which men behave as distinct from their rationale of their behavior, do we in fact find evidence for the existence of a common good or a general will? And, further, if the state is an association among others,

CONCLUSION

or an organization, does the myth of the social contract express anything about the nature of the state which is not true of all other associations and hence differentiates the state from them? If sufficient reasons can be adduced for answering these questions in the negative, we can conclude that there is nothing in the facts that forces us to set up as basic and distinctive in a theory of the state either a common good, or a general will, or a social contract. If it is still felt necessary to postulate one or more of these concepts, we can be sure that some other reason —rationalization of political programs, traditional ways of thinking, justification of some exercise of power—lies at the bottom of it.

A common good, one which when realized will benefit a number of people, is usually the aim, if not the result, of coöperative action.[6] Coöperative action is the foundation of any association. In order to use common good as a differentia of the state, it is necessary to show first that such a common good exists and, second, that there is something about the common good of the state that marks it off as more inclusive or more vital or at least different from the common goods of other associations. Those who have tried have found it difficult to give a consistent account of what the common good of the state is.[7] Concerning the second point we must ask: has this in fact been shown? According to some theories, the common good of the state is self-realization of all its members.[8] Unless we are willing to hold that the state includes all other associations (and in that event there ceases to be a problem

---

[6] The distinction between "common" and "like" goods does not seem relevant here.

[7] Chamberlain, *The American Stakes*, p. 152.

[8] I am not here considering the validity of the concept of self-realization.

CONCLUSION

of sovereignty, indeed there ceases to be any political problem), we must recognize that many individuals find their self-realization in nonpolitical forms of activity.[9] In Laski's earlier writings we find a forceful presentation of this point. According to another version of this theory, the common good of the state is the maintenance of the conditions of self-realization. Such a theory, even if it has inner consistency, has two weaknesses. First, it fails as a basis of a theory of sovereignty, inasmuch as it attributes a negative character to all state actions. Secondly, in so doing it disregards the facts of state action as we know them today. If we consider government as the agent, or representative, of the state, as the idealistic thinkers do, we find the state, through government, engaged in many practices which can in no sense be called negative. Close to this theory is that which holds that the common good which is at the basis of sovereignty is peace. This is the view held by Machiavelli and Hobbes in the classical tradition and by the legal realists more recently. That peace is desired by most men cannot be doubted. But merely to say that the sovereignty of the state rests on its securing peace is not sufficient. The methods by which that peace is secured are all-important. Do they involve a suppression of all disagreement with and criticism of the government? Or must we assume that methods are to be available for meeting criticism and resolving conflicts? If the former, if peace is obtained at the price of freedom, it is really subjection or slavery and implies no common good. If the latter, an elaboration of the technique of securing peace without destroying freedom is required. If we say no more than that the common good

[9] The same criticism holds for the Utilitarian point of view which differs on this point more in terminology than in consequences.

CONCLUSION

of the state is peace, what we are saying is that government is necessary. In that sense the justification of government is that it governs. But the concept of peace, as it will be used below, is more than that, since it involves the problem of freedom. It means not only control by subjection, which does not end conflict (it merely *suppresses* it) but also a technique of conciliation which recognizes claims and attempts to judge them. This is the kind of peace that is necessary for freedom and that is commonly denoted by equity. It is freedom as well as equity, because after such judgment interests that were previously frustrated are now aware of the limits within which they may proceed in peace. Finally, we find advanced as the common good of the state, justice or the rule of law. In one sense this is merely a restatement of the peace theory and is subject to the same objections. It can be said to differ from that view, since it considers the state as essentially legal and comes to the position that sovereignty belongs to the judiciary as the interpreters of the law. Sovereignty in this sense ceases to be a political term and, quite rightly, becomes merely a point of reference in a legal structure. This is the essence of the Austinian theory of sovereignty which brings it down to a matter of law and says that the highest point in the legal structure, that which gives commands, but does not receive them, is sovereign. This general view has had various emphases. Hobbes attributed sovereignty to the executive, Austin to the legislature. In the United States the holders of this position might point to the judiciary —in the last analysis, the Supreme Court. However, the difficulty in taking this view too literally is that investigation indicates that it is often almost impossible to find the sovereign. Furthermore, the unity of the legal struc-

CONCLUSION

ture, which has long been a principle of law, does not guarantee the unity of society in the state, since law is only a particular aspect of the state.

The inadequacy of these arguments for a common good undermines the general will as well, since the essence of the general will theory is that the general will is that will which wills the common good. If there is no common good, there can be no general will. That the overwhelming majority of the people may be agreed on a particular point at a particular time, proves nothing, inasmuch as this merely represents a sum of like desires or interests, which is very different from what a general will is meant to be.

If after rejecting the common good and the general will as foundations of the unity of the state we turn to social contract, conceived as a unitary system of obligation rather than of common ends, we have the same sort of question to ask. What is there about the idea of social contract when used in connection with the state that differentiates it from the social contracts or agreements involved in the obligations toward other associations? Some of the earlier contract theorists would not recognize the existence of other associations, "like wormes in the entrayles of a natural man," according to Hobbes.[10] The growth of associations, in spite of Hobbes's warning, did weaken the state, thereby proving, or at least promoting, Hobbes's point. For this reason the contract theory has been continually restated in various forms. The way in which the state is distinguished from other associations in the pluralistic restatement of this theory is in the degree, or rather special kind, of power given up to the state. To the state alone, it is asserted, is given the power of

[10] *Leviathan,* chap. xxix.

CONCLUSION

coercion or the use of force to enforce its commands. This is true in the case of no other association, and it puts the state above all other associations in power. The validity of this argument depends upon whether physical force is the most effective or ultimate form of coercion. For a man of Hobbes's temperament it certainly was, but the peculiarity of Hobbes's character is what disproves the argument. For most men there are more pervasive powers than the police. The power to coerce has often been less effective than the "inducements" of the church or the employer.[11] Even if we grant the uniqueness of the "association of coercion," it is still necessary to recognize that such an association may divide more than it unifies and hence cannot be relied on (even by the state) as the supreme form of unity.

It may still be argued that, although the possession of force does not put the state above other associations as a supreme force of power, it does distinguish the state from them. This is certainly true formally, but in practice such coercion is not easily defined. The so-called inducements of other associations are often difficult to distinguish from the coercion of the police, being no less resented as punishments and being in effect compulsory. The purpose of the social contract theory was to establish a unified law (see Hobbes, Spinoza, and Rousseau). It has been shown that the law is only one kind of control among other kinds even when it has its peculiar techniques and that even the most unified structure of contracts and obligations does not suffice to create the organic social unity implied by "the Leviathan."

[11] On the latter point see Hale, "Force and the State: a comparison of 'political' and 'economic' compulsion," *Columbia Law Review*, XXXV (Feb., 1935), 149–201.

CONCLUSION

The discussion thus far has attempted to show that in light of recent social changes, especially the growth of power of nonpolitical associations, the old arguments for the unity of the state and its all-inclusive or superior character must be rejected.

Observation shows us an infinite diversity in the contents of wills, not only as to practical content but also as to the ideals aimed at for one's self and for others. And hence it would seem to be fundamentally erroneous to suppose some preestablished harmony between the wills of men as touching what they will.[12]

It is in the light of these conditions that we must again turn to the question of the nature and the function of the state, bearing in mind the general problem of self-government, namely, the establishing of freedom within a framework of order. A political theory which attempts to take into consideration all forms of social organization and which denies the unity of society in a common good or a general will, proceeds more fruitfully by using the term "government" instead of the term "state." The term "government" does not carry over the connotation of unity which has been attached to the term "state." Government is the function of bringing some kind of order into that which is essentially unordered. Government is of the community rather than of the state. A community needs ordering. The idea of the state carries the assumption of order, begging the question of government.

It is in terms of this problem of government that I wish to consider briefly one remaining view of social unity, which differs from these others in that it has not been the basis of a special doctrine of sovereignty. This

[12] Catlin, *Principles of Politics,* p. 153. By permission of The Macmillan Company, publishers.

CONCLUSION

view was put most briefly in the famous statement of Lord Balfour. "Our whole political machinery presupposes a people so fundamentally at one that they can safely afford to bicker." [13] What it means to be "fundamentally at one" is difficult to say. C. J. Friedrich has attempted to show that the essence of the democratic state is that we recognize that we are not fundamentally at one, but are willing to get things done by compromise.[14] This forces the supporters of the Balfour doctrine back to the view that at least we agree to differ. But this is scarcely a sufficient account of the kind of unity on which the state can be founded. Balfour's statement may be interpreted as claiming that in order that a political system may work, there must be some fundamental agreement to tolerate plurality. Admitting a diversity of ends and wills, there must be unity as to what kind of means will be permitted regardless of the ends in view. In other words, there must be an agreement not to use disruptive means. This might be called a theory of "common means" as over against the theory of the common end. Such a theory runs into all the difficulties that confront any rigid separation of means and end, and dialectitians will point out that certain "means" are thus transformed into ends. The practical difficulty, however, with such a theory is that it interprets law as merely a technique for limiting conflict and that in essence it does not differ from the social contract or "peace" theory criticized above.

These criticisms, suggested by the pluralistic approach to the problem of the state, were not carried out thoroughly by any of the pluralists considered. They were

[13] Introduction to "World Classics" edition of Bagehot, *The English Constitution*, p. xxiv.
[14] "Democracy and dissent," *Political Quarterly*, X (Oct., 1939), 571–82.

CONCLUSION

content, first, to deny sovereignty and, second, to discredit the state in favor of some other association. The three men with whom we have been chiefly concerned here clearly failed to get at the roots of sovereignty and failed also in their attempts to discredit the state. Figgis, limited by his special interest, in the end fell back on Gierke's version of the organic theory. Cole's interest in the economic problem led him to suggest the erection of a gigantic economic organization, the co-ordinating body of which can hardly be distinguished from the sovereign state. Laski, most violent in his attacks on sovereignty and monism in general, first advocated a pluralistic sovereignty and later a view of the state which was Marxian in terminology and idealistic in content. The failure of the pluralists to develop an adequate theory of the nature of the state was the chief vulnerable point for the critics of pluralism. The difficulty was that the pluralists discredited the state to further some particular interest rather than to develop a more adequate political theory. If we bear in mind the motivation of the pluralists (chiefly moral), we may now ask the positive question: What is the significance of the pluralistic approach, conceived as a clarification of the social conditions under which government and freedom operate, for a positive theory of the free state which is compatible with modern social complexities?

Using Balfour's view as a point of departure, we can reply to him as follows: There is something in the contention that community is possible only in view of the fact that not all interests are at stake in any one quarrel, but it is wrong to assume that there is any basic or underlying interest. If we omit the question as to what is fundamental, we may revise Balfour's statement to this: In or-

CONCLUSION

der to be able to quarrel safely on one point, we must be in agreement on some other point. If this were not the case, our quarrel would cleave society in two and thus destroy it, since we would have no reason for wanting to settle. This view would lead to such statements as, in order to quarrel on political matters, we must be at one on economic matters, or religious matters, and so forth. Yet even this is not accurate, because as a matter of fact we argue about many matters all the time. What really happens is that our other interests keep our tendency to go to extremes for any one interest in check.[15] It is the realization of this fact that makes it possible to propose the following answer to the problem of unity. What holds a society together, in spite of the numerous conflicts which arise among individuals and groups in it, is the fact that these individuals and groups have other interests which are so important to them that they hesitate to go to extremes in any one particular conflict.[16] The breakdown of society is caused by conflicts between individuals who

[15] Compare the following: "Thus the citizen who is not identified with a party, who does not habitually participate in politics, and whose support cannot be counted upon by any one group, is the agent that keeps politicians uncertain of their power and therefore responsive to the current of opinion. If all men were good citizens in the sense of being participants in all contests they would have to act in practice like declared partisans. This would bring too many political contests to a danger point of intensity."—Herring, *The Politics of Democracy*, pp. 32–33.

[16] "At first sight it might seem that the conflicting interests of two communities must be more easily adjusted than the rival claims of a larger number. It would appear, however, that the reverse proposition is more nearly true. In a union of two powers there can hardly fail to be a direct feeling of rivalry, and the continuing suspicion either on the one side or the other that the balance is not truly held. But in a polity constructed out of many states or provinces such a feeling is greatly diluted. Indeed, the more complex the interplay of material, religious, and political interests, the more easy is it to discover and maintain a stable political combination. . . . The consolidating influence of multiplicity . . ."—Fisher, *Political Unions*, pp. 16–17.

CONCLUSION

are members of only one group,[17] whose whole personality is bound up in that group, or by conflicts which are felt to be so basic that all other interests are sacrificed. It is the attitude of the people concerned toward a given interest that determines whether it is basic. Usually no interest is so basic that it is not submitted to some sort of arbitration or judgment. The final paragraph of the *Communist Manifesto* of Marx and Engels suggests that the proletariat as a class have no stakes in society and hence have nothing to lose by violent revolution. On the contrary, few persons are in fact so desperate or so single-minded. Most of us most of the time have something to lose, if only our lives, and we hesitate to throw our many interests into one supreme issue.

Up to this point the argument has attempted to clear up the problem of the basis of the unity of social life without assuming any unity in the sense of common good or aim. It has been shown that it is possible to base the essential unity on "the consolidating influence of multiplicity," that is, on a multiplicity of interests, and hence on a multiplicity of associations, and that the erection of a hierarchy of associations is unnecessary. If different men were members of different associations, that is, if there were no overlapping memberships, and if, furthermore, each man were a member of only one association, or if there were a large majority or the most energetic portion of the community who belonged to only one association, such unity as has been described—community, or, to use the language of the idealists, *negative* unity—would be impossible or un-

[17] Lowell calls these "irreconcilables."—*Public Opinion and Popular Government*, p. 32.

CONCLUSION

desirable.[18] It is only because all men, or nearly all men, are members of several associations as a result of their having several interests that community is possible. A theory of unity on the basis of universal agreement on one end for the whole society is comparatively simple. Such is the unity of the totalitarian states and of states at war or in an "emergency" in general. In such cases there is no problem of freedom or of equilibrium, for the majority of the people, those doing what they want to do and those submitting to that which they must do, are free to fight and possibly are fighting for freedom; otherwise they cannot hope to enjoy freedom for the present. The problem of freedom and equilibrium arises in the pluralistic situation which I have described. It is in the multiplicity of interrelated interests and the plurality of overlapping groups that the unity of a peaceful democratic community is to be found.

It is also in this situation that the problems of the nature of government and democracy become crucial. Granted the assumption of the totalitarian state, universal support for the leader and unanimity of aim, talk about freedom becomes meaningless. The problem of government is merely that of the fastest means of achieving the common aim. In the community where a variety of interests is recognized, however, such as the community of the liberal democratic country, it becomes extremely important to discover the particular and shifting aims and problems of community government—not merely to make that government efficient. In a pluralistic

[18] This was the situation of the members of the Communist and National Socialist parties in Germany during the latter period of the Weimar Republic.—Watkins, *The Failure of the Constitutional Emergency Powers under the German Republic*, pp. 88 ff.

CONCLUSION

society the government is seldom a leader; when it is, it leads in very limited fields.

Prior to any discussion of the various kinds of freedom in the community, it is necessary to consider the question of government [19] in its broadest terms. Government may be the administration of a group interest, the function of carrying out plans of coöperative action, the administration of shared policies. The function of government is to be found both in single groups and in pluralistic communities. (1) If the group consists of a number of people coöperating for the achievement of a common good, the problem of democratic government is relatively clear. How can the views and desires of the members of the group on the question of the means of achieving the end in view be fulfilled with the maximum possible efficiency of the administration of the group? Here the common good, which is the basis of the unity of the group, has a positive content; for example, in the church salvation and in the business corporation profits. Insofar as the groups are not compulsory, the problem of freedom is replaced by the problem of effective representation and efficient administration.

(2) The community, however, is not such a group, but the matrix in which groups operate. Morris Ginsberg has described it as follows:

Modern society is especially characterized by the complexity of its publics, and a proper understanding of their relations to one another and to the institutions and associations to which they give rise is essential in order to get a real grasp of the nature of public opinion. We have seen that the conception of organism and mind alike exaggerate the unity of the community. The latter consists of a series of groupings, partly

---

[19] On the preference of the term "government" over the term "state" see Dewey, *The Public and Its Problems*, pp. 8–9.

CONCLUSION

coincident, partly divergent, and best represented as a series of circles some of which are concentric whilst others cut across each other. Individuals may and do belong to many of these circles or groupings and the closeness of their relations to them varies enormously. Moreover the groupings themselves are not fixed, but are in a state of flux and subject to constant motion and transformation. Within each of the groupings there is a mass of operative ideas and sentiments, the result of a process of communication and reciprocal influence. Within each there grow up associations, i. e. organizations for securing common ends and institutions, i. e. definite or sanctioned or crystallized modes of relationship between members of the group. The group, however, always retains within itself more than can be expressed in its associations and institutions.[20]

The case of government in the community, political government, is more complicated and must be distinguished from the administration of group objectives, since it must take into consideration the existence side by side of groups with conflicting interests and since there is no clearly defined common good or general interest. Furthermore, since membership in a community is to all intents and purposes compulsory, a discussion of the nature of political freedom involves additional problems and must be carried on in different terms from that of the freedom of group life. If government is the carrying out of plans of action, in the case of the community, since there is no positive good stated, we must ask, plans of action with regard to what? In formal terms we must seek to define those functions which are communal or public by nature, if by "public" we mean those functions which are the concern, and by their nature must be the concern, not of any voluntary group, but of the community.

An attack on this problem has been made by Dewey in

[20] *The Psychology of Society*, pp. 138–39.

CONCLUSION

The Public and Its Problems. In Lippmann's *The Phantom Public,* which was the immediate occasion of Dewey's critique, the public is that group of people who are outside any particular conflict. This puts the public at a disadvantage in dealing with a conflict, as compared with the "insiders." Only in a serious case can it step in to show where its sympathy lies. It is, thus, a nebulous group, variable in size and composition, unstable and irregular in activity, and, above all, unorganized. Dewey [21] on the other hand, conceives the public as stable and continuous, holding that the state is the public as organized and articulated through officials. "Indirect, extensive, enduring and serious consequences of conjoint and interacting behavior call a public into existence having a common interest in controlling these consequences."[22] Although Dewey uses the expression a "common interest" in this passage and throughout the book, it is by no means the same thing as the common good which was criticized above. Here the common interest is a particular type of concern,[23] distinguished from the "common good" of any group; it is a public interest in any problem. It is the indirect consequences of interrelated group activities which determine the common interest relative to a particular issue, not the common good which determines the public problems. In this formulation the positive question is: How do we determine which problems are communal? A formal answer to this question has already been suggested. Those problems are communal which cannot be completely handled by any or by all the parties directly concerned in a conflict. That answer springs from the definition of "community." What specific problems

[21] *Op. cit.,* p. 67.   [22] *Ibid.,* p. 126.
[23] Compare with Cole's view, *supra,* pp. 44–45.

CONCLUSION

are in fact communal depends on the knowledge of the consequences of individual and social behavior possessed at the period under consideration.[24] The history of so-called "social legislation" is an excellent example of the growing awareness on the part of the community of the consequences of the growth of industry under a laissez faire policy of government.

If we ask what distinguishes government of a community from all other government, it is the fact that since a community is "compulsory" (members cannot leave it readily), it has the additional problem of making a single set of rules for people who, because they disagree on most matters, need a conventional procedure for discovering the public consequences of private conflicts.[25] The necessity of a single set of rules originates in no natural law, supernatural function, or ultimate good, but simply from the fact that public problems are such that a unified administration is the only type of administration that is practicable. This is the only practical meaning of the concept of sovereignty.

Granted the validity of this account of the nature of communal or public interests and problems, we can in these terms discuss the functions of government and the conditions of freedom. If in general we can say that government deals with the problems that arise from the fact that men live in groups and pursue their different ways of life in different groups, and that each of these groups has contacts with other groups, we can by observation distinguish two techniques made use of by government

[24] Compare with the analysis of Laski's view of rights, *supra*, p. 55.
[25] "The politico-economic system depends on conformity. In any community there can be only one effective code of law, one state, one constitution, one form of currency, one contractual order."—MacIver, *Leviathan and the People*, pp. 139–40.

CONCLUSION

for dealing with these problems. Each of these techniques has a long history, and each is adapted to a certain kind of problem. In the first category are those problems which are stabilized or which refer to traditionally accepted norms or formally enacted plans of action. These problems are handled by the courts operating within the legal structure of government. What is known as the common law is the accretion of the results of numerous attempts to settle these problems (conflicts) with a minimum of friction and general disturbance in the community. The relative stability of a community is indicated by the ratio of the number of communal problems handled by the courts to the total number of such problems. A community without courts is likely to be a highly unstable community. A community in which most problems are handled by the courts is referred to as having a government of laws as distinguished from a government of men.

In the second place, there are new problems, problems raised by developments in the fields of economics, religion, and so forth, whose communal character has just been detected, and also problems which, though they are traditional, are variable in that they periodically take on new aspects. Modern constitutional governments have made provision for dealing with these problems. They are dealt with through conferences, codes, politics, legislation, collective bargaining, and so forth. That no hard and fast line can be drawn between the first type and the second is indicated by the current discussion concerning the status of administrative tribunals. The existence of these tribunals merely indicates the gradual stereotyping of the problems with which they are concerned.

Turning from the problems to a consideration of gov-

CONCLUSION

ernment, we can make the following distinctions between the courts, on the one hand, and politics and legislation, on the other. (1) Courts are nonpartisan, they deal with traditional problems, and they imply some sort of unified legal structure. Insofar as society is monistic, its unity is represented by the continual attempt on the part of the judges and jurists to show the harmony and completeness of the legal system by attempting to make every decision fit in with all the rest. (2) Politics and legislation are partisan in that they have involved the existence of parties; they deal with new and changing issues and hence must be more plastic; and any unity is achieved with greater difficulty and likely to be less permanent.

In the case of group life freedom is secured by the existence for the individual of many alternative choices as to what to do and how to do it. In the sphere of the relation of the groups to each other and to the community, the sphere of politics proper, freedom is measured by the extent to which one group affects the interests of another. It is a different kind of freedom, and the means of achieving it to a greater or lesser degree are comprised in what has come to be known as "pressure politics." "Pressure politics" is a realistic substitute for the classic attempts to define "equal" liberties or rights. Freedom is not based on equal liberties, but on "elbow room," on the ability to pursue a particular interest without "pressing" on others hard enough to arouse "public" coercion or pressure.

An elaboration of how freedom is achieved for groups in communities by politics requires the elaboration of a theory of the nature and function of political parties. The activity of "pressure politics," especially in connec-

CONCLUSION

tion with legislation and administration, generates what may be termed "public groups," commonly known as "political parties." The plurality of political parties is the device by means of which the necessities of political government are tempered by organizing rival public interests. Instead of having competing governments within the community, political parties are formed in order to permit the expression of competing views as to what government should do and how it should do it. Political parties are the organized "publics" in the community.[26]

The situation may be described as follows: On the one hand we find groups with particular interests; on the other, political parties which singly or in coalition run the government.[27] These parties can have at least two relations to the groups in society, corresponding to which there are two theories of political parties. (1) Each party may represent a specific interest, and a coalition of special interests forms the public government. Such parties are traditionally called factions or lobbies, and, if they represent special functions, would exist in a system of functional representation such as Cole outlined. (2) According to the other theory each party represents public policy for an aggregate of interests focused upon certain issues of government which at the time are considered to be of major importance. Thus, in this country the Democratic Party may be backed by labor unions, farmer groups, and other "factions," while the Republican Party may be supported by Chambers of Commerce, small busi-

---

[26] "The lasting, extensive, enduring and serious consequences of conjoint and interacting behavior" bring into existence not "a public" as Dewey would have it, but a plurality of publics organized as political parties. In Dewey the relation between political groups and the public is not clear.—*Op. cit.*, pp. 35, 67; see also Jenks, *The State and the Nation*, p. 196: ". . . the aims of a party are *public*."

[27] Herring, *op. cit.*, p. 120 ff.

CONCLUSION

ness men's groups, and other special interests.[28] But if the party is the tool of these lobbies, it is not a genuine party (in this second sense). It must be the expression of "public opinion," each party representing a public, that is, a number of citizens, belonging to many groups, with a definite view as to what should be done about public problems and how it should be done. A party in this sense is a pluralistic "general will."

Looking at the present state of affairs in England and America, the two large nations where popular government has run a free course for the greatest length of time, we are justified in saying that the existence of parties is not mainly due to differences of temperament, to conflicting interests, or to the basic forces that create variations of opinion and emotion in mankind, but that they are rather agencies whereby public attention is brought to a focus on certain questions that must be decided. They have become instruments for carrying on popular government by concentrating opinion. Their function is to make the candidates and issues known and to draw the people together into large masses, so that they can speak with a united voice, instead of uttering an unintelligible babel of discordant cries. In short, their service in politics is largely advertisement and brokerage.[29]

The modern legislator, instead of finding himself the representative of merely a single geographical area, finds that in order to accomplish his purposes he must take into consideration these occupational groupings. Mr. A, Congressman from the first district in Pennsylvania or Illinois, soon finds it advisable to ally himself with the Federation or the Chamber, or some other social or economic group. There is scarcely an interest of the section of the country from which he comes that can today be satisfied without the help and support of a group organized on a national scale. Instead of being the

---
[28] Laski, *The American Presidency*, p. 160; Jennings, *Parliament*, pp. 127–28.
[29] Lowell, *Public Opinion and Popular Government*, pp. 65–66.

CONCLUSION

representative of his district solely, he becomes of necessity the representative of particular economic and social groups.[30]

Political action—the behavior of the citizen—does not occur as a pure element in the social world. Men find their interest in the political process, and their civic behavior is determined by their connections with churches, labor unions, business associations, fraternal organizations, and so on. As political issues involve industry, labor, social status, or religion, they bring about the intervention of men whose welfare is involved through common concern with these problems.[31]

These three quotations touch upon the issue from the point of view of political parties, the legislator, and the citizen; but none of them explicitly conceives political parties as publics.

Once an election has taken place and the majority of the citizens have decided which party they want to run the government, we find the two parties in opposite situations. One holds the power in the Legislature and the key positions in the Executive. This party, which is said to be in office, has the responsibility of running the government, that is, of solving the public problems as it sees them. The other party, usually retaining the support of the individuals and groups that backed it at the election, has no less a public "office" or responsibility of criticizing the policies of the elected party and thereby of keeping before the citizens the central issues of government, what the party in power is doing about them, and what they themselves would do if elected. This description of the operation of the party system is more applicable to the English government than to the American. In England, in normal times, the major portion of the votes are party

[30] Childs, *Labor and Capital in National Politics*, p. 250.
[31] Herring, *op. cit.*, p. 34.

CONCLUSION

votes. In the United States, the rigidity of the government (the secure position of the Executive and the set term of office for the members of the Legislature) is compensated for by the relative weakness of the party hold on members of the Legislature on specific issues. In this way the party system is a technique of political freedom, inasmuch as through the opposition party's activity the citizens can know the harmful results of the government policy and can exercise control over the government at the next election.

But the party system is more than a system of freedom, it is a form of government. It is that form of government which can effectively take into consideration the interests and desires of the citizens in formulating public policy. The party system is the most satisfactory device thus far invented by means of which the many interests in the community can be effectively organized for changes in public policy.[32] Since public problems are for the most part conflicts arising from the diversity of interests in the community, the functions of parties are here viewed as more than judicial. Lippmann's restatement of republicanism is inadequate:

So we must ask ourselves what is the true function of the official. We have defined the liberal state as one in which social control is achieved mainly by administering justice among men rather than by administering men and their affairs by overhead authority. It follows that the temper of officialdom in a liberal society must be *predominantly* judicial: that holds not only for the judges themselves but for the legislators and executives as well, indeed for all who wish to serve the public interest. Except, of course, in emergencies

---

[32] Childs indicates that the party is not the only device for the furthering of the policy of interest groups. The groups themselves have direct contact with government (*op. cit.*, pp. 243 ff.).

CONCLUSION

when a community must temporarily renounce its freedom in order to defend itself against attack, upheaval, and disaster, the primary task of liberal statesmanship is to judge the claims of particular interests asking a revision of laws, and to endeavor amidst these conflicting claims to make equitable decisions.[33]

The party must subordinate judgment to the formation of policy; it must transform judicial decision into "good judgment."

If we approach freedom from the point of view of the individual, in the manner of Mill, we find that our problem is set in terms of the dialectic of the individual and society. It was the contribution of the pluralists to the analysis of freedom to show that the use of the term "society" was an oversimplification which led, on the one hand, to the view which set the individual against "society" and, on the other hand, to the neglect of the complicated forms of behavior which are included in the term "society." Man's freedom is not to be gained from society, but is to be achieved in society. The consideration of Figgis enabled us to see the nature of freedom in society, social freedom. The analyses of Cole and Laski made clear the problems raised by the conflict between the desire for social freedom and the necessity for economic and political action.

The conclusion of this essay is that the nature of freedom can be discussed more adequately on the basis of a distinction between social freedom (freedom in the community) and political freedom (freedom for parties). It was pointed out that certain phases of community life admit of a maximum of freedom, namely, the existence of a multiplicity of competing groups. This may be called

[33] Lippmann, *The Good Society*, pp. 284–85.

CONCLUSION

the ideal condition of freedom. That this freedom is not absolute does not mean that it is nonexistent. The essence of this social freedom has been summed up by Unwin in the following terms:

> But what do I mean by thus setting off Society as against the State? Do they represent opposite forces? In a sense they do, though this is not often realized. I mean by the State that one of our social cohesions which has drawn to itself the exercise of final authority and which can support that authority, if need be, with the sanction of physical force. And I mean by Society all the rest of our social cohesions—family, trade-union, church, and the rest. Now human progress and human liberty have depended and continue to depend on the multiplication of our social cohesions, and on the withdrawal of final authority and of the sanction of force from all our social cohesions except one—the State. Primitive man was restricted to a single social cohesion, which controlled him with supreme authority. Life was impossible outside his tribe. Freedom was impossible within it. The great array of differentiated social cohesions, which represent in their totality the free Society of modern civilization, and from which the authority and force embodied in the State have withdrawn themselves, furnish the individual with that great variety of choice which constitutes real freedom.[34]

The necessity for having one political administration limits the scope of freedom in the political sphere. Instead of competing political associations, the mechanism of political freedom is the existence of competing parties taking turns in the control of the political association. Rarely does one party win a complete victory. Democratic government involves the existence of an opposition. Cole's mistake was that he failed to see this and to take it into account in his theory of Guild Socialism.

[34] Unwin, "Thoughts on Society and the State," in *Studies in Economic History*, p. 458. By permission of The Macmillan Company, publishers.

CONCLUSION

The freedom to join another group that is characteristic of social freedom is replaced by the freedom to criticize and the freedom to appeal, at certain intervals, to the citizens for support in the struggle to control the government.

The situation that democracy recognizes as the setting of its problems is what has been called cultural pluralism—the existence of diverse ways of life practiced by various groups in the same community. Democracy solves the problem of freedom by recognizing and permitting the existence of this cultural pluralism, restricting its regulating function solely to those actions of the group which raise communal problems. Even in this case democracy attempts to preserve what freedom is possible under the exigencies of government, by formulating its policies through political parties on the basis of these various interest groups.

General unity is neither the condition nor the aim of democracy. It is occasionally a necessity under certain conditions and in certain spheres. In times of war all governments, even democracies, tend to become totalitarian. However, if we grant the existence of peace, we may say that democracy attempts to operate on a minimum of unity, using the political process to close up dangerous gaps when they appear. In the administration of the law of any country a unified legal system is necessary. The unity of the legal system, however, is not socially constitutive, but is merely a political instrument for dealing with basic plurality. The Constitution is not basic socially: it is "federal" in more senses than one. By means of it many varied interests are held in "federal" equilibrium without being united in aim or in method.

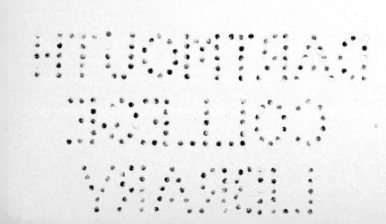

BIBLIOGRAPHY

Arnold, T. W., The Symbols of Government. New Haven, Yale University Press, 1935.
Ascoli, Max, and Fritz Lehman, eds., Political and Economic Democracy. New York, Norton, 1937.
Barker, Ernest, "The Discredited State," *Political Quarterly*, No. 5 (Feb., 1915), 101–21. Reprinted in Ernest Barker, Church, State and Study, London, Methuen, 1930.
—— Political Thought in England from Herbert Spencer to the Present Day. New York, Holt, 1915.
Bosanquet, Bernard, The Philosophical Theory of the State. London, Macmillan, 1910.
Catlin, G. E. G., Principles of Politics. New York, Macmillan, 1930.
Chamberlain, John, The American Stakes. New York, Carrick and Evans, 1940.
Childs, H. L., Labor and Capital in National Politics. Columbus, Ohio State University, 1930.
Cohen, H. E., Recent Theories of Sovereignty. Chicago, University of Chicago Press, 1937.
Coker, F. W., "Pluralistic Theories and the Attack upon State Sovereignty," in Merriam and Barnes, Political Theories, Recent Times. New York, Macmillan, 1924.
—— Recent Political Thought. New York, Appleton-Century, 1934.
Cole, G. D. H., Guild Socialism. London, The Fabian Society, 1920. "Fabian Tract" 192.
—— Guild Socialism Re-stated. London, Parsons, 1920.
—— Social Theory. New York, Stokes, 1920.

BIBLIOGRAPHY

Dewey, John, The Public and Its Problems. New York, Holt, 1927.
—— Freedom and Culture. New York, Putnam, 1939.
Elliott, W. Y., Pragmatic Revolt in Politics. New York, Macmillan, 1928.
Ellis, E. D., "Guild Socialism and Pluralism," *American Political Science Review,* XVII (Nov., 1923), 584–96.
—— "The Pluralistic State," *American Political Science Review,* XIV (Aug., 1920), 393–407.
Figgis, J. N., Churches in the Modern State. London, Longmans, 1914.
—— The Fellowship of the Mystery. London, Longmans, 1914.
Fisher, H. A. L., Political Unions. Oxford, Clarendon Press, 1911.
Friedrich, C. J., "Democracy and Dissent," *Political Quarterly,* X (Oct., 1939), 571–82.
Ginsberg, Morris, "Is There a General Will?" in Proceedings of the Aristotelian Society, XX (1919–20), 89–112.
—— The Psychology of Society. London, Methuen, 1921.
Green, T. H., Lectures on the Principles of Political Obligation. New York and London, Longmans, 1885.
Hale, R. L., "Force and the State: a comparison of 'political' and 'economic' compulsion," *Columbia Law Review,* XXXV (Feb., 1935), 149–201.
Herring, Pendleton, The Politics of Democracy. New York, Norton, 1940.
Hobhouse, L. T., The Metaphysical Theory of the State. London, Allen and Unwin, 1918.
—— The Rational Good. London, Allen and Unwin, 1921.
Hobson, S. G., National Guilds and the State. London, Bell, 1920.
Hsiao, K. C., Political Pluralism; a study in contemporary political theory. London, Kegan, Paul, Trench, Trubner, 1927.
Jenks, E., The State and the Nation. London, Dent, 1919.
Jennings, W. I., Parliament. New York, Macmillan, 1940.
Laski, H. J., Problem of Sovereignty. New Haven, Yale University Press, 1917.

BIBLIOGRAPHY

Laski, H. J., Authority in the Modern State. New Haven, Yale University Press, 1919.
—— Foundations of Sovereignty. New York, Harcourt, Brace, 1921.
—— The State in the New Social Order. London, The Fabian Society, 1922. "Fabian Tract" 200.
—— Grammar of Politics. New Haven, Yale University Press, 1925.
—— An Introduction to Politics. London, Allen and Unwin, 1931.
—— Democracy in Crisis. Chapel Hill, University of North Carolina Press, 1933.
—— Liberty in the Modern State. London, Faber, 1930.
—— Studies in Law and Politics. New Haven, Yale University Press, 1932.
—— The State in Theory and Practice. New York, Viking Press, 1935.
—— Parliamentary Government in England. New York, Viking Press, 1938.
—— The Prospects of Democratic Government, "Bulletin of the College of William and Mary," XXXIII, No. 4 (April, 1939).
—— "The Obsolescence of Federalism," *New Republic*, XCVIII (May 3, 1939), 367–69.
—— The Danger of Being a Gentleman. New York, Viking Press, 1940.
—— The American Presidency. New York and London, Harper, 1940.
Lewis, J. D., The Genossenschaft-Theorie of Otto von Gierke. Madison, 1935. "University of Wisconsin Studies in the Social Sciences," 25.
Lindsay, A. D., "The State in Recent Political Theory," *Political Quarterly*, No. 1 (Feb., 1914), 128–45.
—— The Essentials of Democracy. Philadelphia, University of Pennsylvania, 1929.
Lippmann, Walter, The Phantom Public. New York, Harcourt, Brace, 1925.
—— The Good Society. Boston, Little, Brown, 1937.

BIBLIOGRAPHY

Lowell, A. L., Public Opinion and Popular Government. New York, Longmans, 1914.

MacIver, R. M., The Modern State. London, Oxford, 1926.

—— Society; Its Structure and Changes. New York, Long and Smith, 1931.

—— Society; a Textbook of Sociology. New York, Farrar, 1937.

—— Leviathan and the People. Louisiana, Louisiana State University Press, 1939.

Maitland, F. W. "Moral Personality and Legal Personality," in Collected Papers, Cambridge, Cambridge University Press, 1911, III, 304–20.

Mannheim, K., Man and Society in an Age of Reconstruction. New York, Harcourt, Brace, 1940.

Merriam, C. E., History of the Theory of Sovereignty since Rousseau. New York, Columbia University Press, 1900.

Mill, J. S. On Liberty. London, Dent (Everyman's ed.), 1910.

Rockow, Lewis, Contemporary Political Thought in England. London, Parsons, 1925.

Rousseau, J.-J., Social Contract. London, Dent (Everyman's ed.), 1923.

Sabine, G. H., "Pluralism: a Point of View," *American Political Science Review*, XVII (Feb., 1923), 34–50.

Schneider, H. W., "Political Implications of Recent Philosophic Movements," in Merriam and Barnes, Political Theories, Recent Times, New York, Macmillan, 1924, pp. 313–56.

Smith, T. V., The Legislative Way of Life. Chicago, University of Chicago Press, 1940.

Tawney, R. H., The Acquisitive Society. London, Bell, 1922.

—— Equality. New York, Harcourt, Brace, 1931.

Unwin, G., Studies in Economic History. London, Macmillan, 1927.

Watkins, F. M., The Failure of Constitutional Emergency Powers under the German Republic. Cambridge, Harvard University Press, 1939.

INDEX

Administrative tribunals, 84
Association: definition, by Cole, 33; true conception of, 13
Associations: source of weakness to state, 72; types of essential, 34; *see also* Groups
Austin, John, 50
Austinianism, 13, 16, 17, 29, 67, 71

Balfour, Arthur James Balfour, Earl of, 75, 76
Barker, Ernest, 6, 22-26, 28-29; "The Discredited State," 22
Bosanquet, Bernard, 6, 50, 54; theory of self-realization, 14, 48
Bradley, F. H., 6, 34
British Labour Party, 47, 57, 59-61

Catlin, G. E. G., *Principles of Politics*, quoted, 74
Childs, H. L., *Labor and Capital in National Politics*, quoted, 87
Church: as true association, 13; relation to state, 19-22, 24
Class struggle, Laski won over to, 57-59
Coercion, basis of state unity, 73
Cole, George Douglas Howard, 63; aim of social organization, 54; association, definition of, 33; attitude toward political parties, 43; contribution to understanding of freedom, 90; economic approach to pluralism, 5; freedom through group representation, 32, 35, 41; functional organization of society, 34 ff.; functional representation for expression of personality, 61; *Guild Socialism*, 33; Guild Socialism, pluralistic theory of, 31-46; *Guild Socialism Restated*, 33, 37, 38, quoted, 39, 40, 41; ignores function of opposition in democracy, 91; implications of social theory, 39-46; nature of human personality, 31; problem of coördination, 37, 76; *Social Theory*, 32, 36, 40, quoted, 33, 34, 37; types of social control, 43-45; view of state, 35 ff.
Common good: attribute of any group, 69; government as administrator for, 80; validity of concept, 68-72
Common interest of public, 82
Common law, 84
Communal problems, 82, 92
Commune, 38
Communist Party, 22
Communitas communitatum, 25, 27
Community, distinguished from group, 81
Consent, relation to sovereignty, 49
Constitution of the United States, 92
Coördination, significance in Cole's theory, 37-39, 44
Courts, function of, 84, 85

INDEX

Democracy: place of opposition in, 91; relation of political to economic, 42; unity not a condition of, 92
Dewey, John, *The Public and Its Problems*, 81
Duty, relation to function, 40

Engels, Friedrich, *see* Marks and Engels

Federalism, Laski on, 59-60
Figgis, John Neville: attacks doctrine of state sovereignty, 15-17, 68, 76; *Churches in the Modern State*, 13, 18, quoted, 26, 29; conception of state, 27-29; contribution to understanding of social freedom, 90; equal importance of groups, 34; *The Fellowship of the Mystery*, quoted, 17, 18; freedom of groups, 13 ff., 32; function of state, 19-22, 26; pluralism of, 10-30; real personality of groups, 16 ff., 54, 61; relevance for political pluralism, 29; religious approach to pluralism, 5
Fisher, H. A. L., *Political Unions*, quoted, 77n
Freedom: Cole's analysis of, 41; based on real personality of groups, 29; conditioned by group activity, 85; distinction between social and political, 90-92; endangered by state centralization, 6; importance in pluralistic theory, 4; pluralism helpful in analyzing, 8; relation to multiplicity of interests, 79; to pluralism, 61; to state-purpose, 55; through decentralization into groups, 17; through sovereignty of people, 67
Freedom of association: Figgis's theory of, 10-30, 32; social implications, 14 ff.

Free Kirk of Scotland, 13
Friedrich, C. J., 75
Functional democracy, 32
Functional organization, Cole's theory, 34 ff.
Functional representation, 35-37, 61

General will, 68, 72
Gierke, Otto von, 3, 16, 27, 55
Ginsberg, Morris, *The Psychology of Society*, quoted, 80
Good life, 54
Government: analysis of authority, 50-53; distinguished from state, 74; function in complex community, 80-83; powers derived from sovereign state, 46; technique for communal problems, 83-85
Greece, city states of, 65
Green, Thomas Hill, 6, 34, 53n; theory of self-realization, 11, 48, 53
Group freedom, Figgis's theory, 32
Groups: ascending hierarchy of, 25, 27, 29; coördination of freedom with other groups, 22; formed for protection against state, 6; functions similar to state, 16; real personality, advisability of recognizing, 17; real personality, criticized by Barker, 22-26; real personality, recognized by Laski, 54; real personality, significance of, 10-30, 61; self-realization, legitimate restrictions on, 24; self-realization related to self-realization of individuals, 12; social implications of freedom of association, 14 ff.; competition of, 54; *see also* Associations
Guild Socialism, 34, 54; Cole's theory of, 31-46; complexity of organization, 42; coördinating

INDEX

agency, 37-39; non-pluralistic view, 45; shifts to monism, 63n

Hegel, Georg Wilhelm Friedrich, 4
Herring, Pendleton, *The Politics of Democracy*, quoted, 77n, 88
Hobbes, Thomas, 70-73 *passim*
Hobhouse, Leonard Trelawney, 54
Hobson, S. G.: *National Guilds and the State*, quoted, 45; theory of guild socialism, 45-46
House of Lords, decision on *Free Church of Scotland Appeals*, 13
Hsiao, K. C., 3

Idealism: built on postulate of unity, 7; theory of the state, 5
Individualism, 7
Individuals, self-realization related to self-realization of groups, 12

James, William, 3
Justice, basis for state sovereignty, 71

Labor, commodity theory of, 39
Laski, Harold Joseph, 8, 9, 63, 76; analysis of power, 56n, 58; conception of state sovereignty, 47-50, 68; concept of state-purpose, 51-53, 55; contribution to understanding of freedom, 90; exponent of individualistic pluralism, 47-62; labor struggle influences thought, 57-59; man as moral agent, 48, 61; moral aspect of governmental authority, 50; "The Obsolescence of Federalism," quoted, 59; political approach to pluralism, 5; *The Problem of Sovereignty*, 47; recognition of group sovereignties, 54, 56; sacrifices pluralism for social reform, 56-60, 62; *The State in Theory and Practice*, 56; theory of the state, 49

Law and order, 25
Legislation, 84, 85
Leo XIII, Encyclical *Immortale Dei*, 3, 21
"Leviathan," 15, 39, 73
Lippmann, Walter: *The Good Society*, quoted, 89; *The Phantom Public*, 82
Lowell, A. L., *Public Opinion and Popular Government*, quoted, 78n, 87

Machiavelli, Niccolò, 70
MacIver, R. M., *The Modern State*, quoted, 27n; *Leviathan and the People*, quoted, 83n
Maitland, Frederic William, 22
Marx, Karl, and Engels, Friedrich, *Communist Manifesto*, 78
Marxism, 56, 58
Mill, John Stuart, 20, 90
Monism, 48, 63n, 64

"Organizing idea," 23-25

Parliamentarianism, Laski's shift to, 62
Party system: as form of government, 89; in England and America, 88
Peace, basis for state sovereignty, 70
Personality, human: Cole's view of, 31; expression through groups, 61
Personality of groups, 10-30, 54
Pluralism: aims, 4-7; analysis, 3; based on observation of facts, 29; exemplified by Cole, 31-46; by Figgis, 10-30; by Laski, 47-62; implications for existing social organization, 46; lines of attack on, 4; more than form of social organization, 64; movement in England, 5-9; not essential to Guild Socialism, 45;

[99]

INDEX

Pluralism: *(continued)*
point of attack on state sovereignty, 67-74; relation to freedom, 61; relevance to present, 8; significance, 3-9, 65; weakness as fighting philosophy, 63
Pluralism, cultural, 92
Pluralism, individualistic, 47-62
Pluralists: contribution to analysis of freedom, 90; ineffectiveness of attack on state sovereignty, 76
Political parties: function, 85-92; ignored by Cole, 43; theories of, 86
Political pluralism, *see* Pluralism
Politics, 84, 85
Power, Laski's analysis of, 56*n*, 58
Pressure politics, 85
Public: definition of, 82; expression through political parties, 86-88

Rights, establishment under state-purpose, 55
Rousseau, Jean Jacques, 73

Self-realization: Figgis's theory of, 11 ff.; Green's theory of, 11
Social contract: basis for state sovereignty, 68; origin, 66; validity of concept, 69, 72-73
Society: Cole's view of, 33; emergence of freedom through, 90
Spencer, Herbert, 6
Spinoza, Baruch, 73
State: actions inside or outside control of, 20; as "organizing idea," 25; as real personality, 26; Cole's definition of, 35, 40; controlled by capitalist class, 58; Hobson's definition of, 45; regulating function, 26-28; relation to church, 19-22, 24
theory of, 5, 66; implications of freedom of association for, 15 ff.; Laski's modification, 49
State-purpose: basis for governmental authority, 51-53; leads to establishment of rights, 55
State sovereignty: moral aspect, 47-50; pluralists' criticism of, 4; pluralists' mode of attack on, 67-74; rejected by Cole, 31, 36, 40; supported by Hobson, 46; practical meaning of, 83; theory developed from state unity, 15; weakness of pluralists' attack on, 76

Tawney, R. H., *The Acquisitive Society*, 40
Totalitarian states, unity in, 79
Trade unions, 22
Tyranny, 18

United Presbyterians of Scotland, 13
Unity, social, 54, 85
Unity, state: basis of, 53, 79; basis of theory of state sovereignty, 15; not a condition of democracy, 92; origin of theory, 66; regarding permissible means, 75; through multiplicity of interests, 77-79
Unwin, G., "Thoughts on Society and the State," quoted, 91
Utilitarian liberalism, 5

Wage slavery, 39
Willoughby, W. W., 46*n*